T0329472

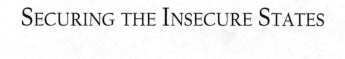

SECURING THE INSECURE STATES

SECURING THE INSECURE STATES IN BRITAIN AND EUROPE

MUSA KHAN JALALZAI

Algora Publishing
New York

Library of Congress Cataloging-in-Publication Data —

Names: Jalalzai, Musa Khan, author.
Title: Securing the insecure states in Britain and Europe/ Musa Khan Jalalzai.
Description: New York: Algora Publishing, [2017] | Includes bibliographical
    references.
Identifiers: LCCN 2017035825 (print) | LCCN 2017037383 (ebook) | ISBN
    9781628943023 (pdf) | ISBN 9781628943009 (soft cover: alk. paper) | ISBN
    9781628943016 (hard cover: alk. paper)
Subjects: LCSH: Terrorism—European Union countries—Prevention. |
    Terrorism—Great Britain—Prevention. | Radicalization—European Union
    countries. | Radicalization—Great Britain.
Classification: LCC HV6433.E85 (ebook) | LCC HV6433.E85 J34 2017 (print) |
    DDC 363.325/16094—dc23
LC record available at https://lccn.loc.gov/2017035825

Printed in the United States

TABLE OF CONTENTS

Introduction

After World War II, certain political and national security experts proposed that forging greater economic and political ties among European countries could reduce the likelihood of future wars. Forty-four years after Britain entered into the EU project, Prime Minister Theresa May triggered Article 50 of the Lisbon Treaty on 29 March 2017. This signaled the first crack in the EU's foundation. A letter invoking Article 50 of the Lisbon Treaty was hand-delivered to the President of the EU, Mr. Donald Tusk, by the UK Ambassador to the European Union, that same day. Experts warned that the UK withdrawal threatens the future of NATO. After the June 2016 vote in favor of Brexit, the UK now feels the impact of its decision. The Prime Minister also warned that, if the EU leaders failed to reach a comprehensive agreement the UK would stop cooperating on law enforcement. But the EU response was also ear-splitting.

Britain originally joined the EC (European Economic Community) in January 1973 and adopted number of treaties to strengthen the integration process. In 1987, the Single European Act set the goal of achieving a unified market by the end of 1992. In 1993, the EU project was established through the Maastricht Treaty. The Treaties of Amsterdam and Nice were reshaped, and the Lisbon Treaty was signed in 2009. In 2013, British Prime Minister demanded negotiation on his country's membership in the EU, while on 17 December 2015; the EU Referendum Act 2015 received the MPs' support that made provision for holding the Brexit referendum in UK and Gibraltar in June 2016.

With the security partnership crumbling at the edges, the Paris, London and Germany terrorist attacks caused dismay across Europe. Insiders who worked in various state and private institutions apparently gave access to sensitive data and intelligence information; this posed a greater threat to the security of all states. It also posed a serious threat to critical infrastructure, nuclear installations, and the defense industry. The British National Security Strategy for 2016–2021 warned that insiders could be a greater threat to national security:

> Of equal concern are those insiders or employees who accidentally cause cyber harm through inadvertent clicking on a phishing email, plugging an infected USB into a computer, or ignoring security procedures and downloading unsafe content from the Internet. Whilst they have no intention of deliberately harming the organization, their privileged access to systems and data mean their action can cause just as much damage as malicious insider.

As extremism and jihadism fuel more and more attacks, law enforcement agencies need to approach local communities, make them vigilant about possible threats and encourage them to share information with the authorities This will help the police in countering terrorism and international organized crime.

The UK law enforcement agencies are in a perilous state, with numerous criminal elements roaming free in towns and cities. Her Majesty's Inspectorate of the Constabulary once warned that criminal cases were being shelved without proper investigation, as police fail to carry out basic functions. All forces in Britain and the EU from counter terrorism policing to secret agencies are struggling to maintain stability in the region, but in spite of all their professional measures and reforms, the threat of lone wolf attacks, organized assaults, and domestic radicalized groups still exists.

CONTEST is Britain's counter terrorism strategy. It was announced in 2003 in response to the exponentially growing jihadist culture. It was revised in 2006, 2009 and 2011, but still is skimpy and sketchy.

On 03 August 2016, Daily Mail reported that Commissioner of Metropolitan Police Sir Bernard Hogan-Howe had unveiled a plan to put professional commandos on patrol — adorned with modern weapons. In major cases, counter-terrorism operations in the UK are being carried out by intelligence-led policing or SO15, which has doubled in size since 2001. Meanwhile, the UK national authority for counter-eavesdropping (NACE) has been focusing on foreign espionage.

The national counter-terrorism security office (NaCTSO) is another police unit that reports to the Home Office. Section 44 of the terrorism act 2000 allows its members to conduct "stop and search." In 2011, when the threat of terrorism and radicalization intensified in London, the Cameron government introduced terrorism prevention and investigation measures (TPIMs) as a replacement for control orders, but recent attacks in London and Manchester have raised some irksome questions about their success.

No doubt, police and counter-terrorism forces in Britain have taken professional measures to counter international terrorism and domestic radicalization, but the core issue they needed to address was the reservation of British communities who have never been disposed to cooperate with law enforcement agencies. Minority communities do not trust or have confidence in the police and security forces, and so they cannot be expected to support counter terror efforts by state agencies. The police reform package of Mr. Tom Winsor also failed due to differences between the police federation and the Home Office.

Criminal and terror suspects continue to dance in the street and towns, disrupting and destroying whatever they want. Some reports confirmed the existence of more than 46,000 wanted criminals and 30,000 jihadist terrorists in England and Wales. Of those, 343 people were sought for murder and 1,012 for rape. Independent police complaints commissions in 2016 reported the investigation of 287 cases of potential police failure. Seemingly every time a terror attack occurs these days, it is said that the suspect was already known to be a risk — yet he was at large, and free to commit murder.

Every year, the Independent Police Complaints Commission investigates thousands of cases of police corruption and complaints about their misconduct, attitude towards communities, and racism, but these and other inquiries never achieved conclusive changes in their attitude. The Leveson Inquiry Report exposed the police department for its malpractices. Former Home Secretary, Theresa May often ordered the Independent Police Complaints Commission (IPCC) to investigate the level of corruption within the police department. Giving evidence to the Leveson hearing, Chief Executive of the IPCC, Jane Furniss revealed that his office received more than

5,179 complaints about the improper disclosure of information by the police between 2006 and 2011. The involvement of both journalists and police officers in serious corruption cases forced former Prime Minister David Cameron to announce a two-part inquiry investigating the role of the press and police in the phone-hacking scandal in July 2011. The Commissioner of London police, Sir Paul Stephenson, was criticized by various quarters about his relationship with the executives of the international news. He failed to explain satisfactorily and resigned on 17 July 2011.

That September, Her Majesty's Inspectorate of Constabulary started investigating corruption allegations against the police and its relationship with media. Former Home Secretary May and Deputy Prime Minister expressed concerns on the public perceptions of police corruption. On 02 March 2017, Her Majesty's Inspector of Constabulary warned that the police were facing crisis of effectiveness, while on 02 April 2016, Express News reported the resignation of 800 police officers due to their failure to deliver. Following the merger of eight regional forces three years ago, another eight hundred constables left their jobs in Scotland.

The UK police face numerous challenges both in policing ethnic communities and in responding to new technological developments, especially in cyberspace. The proliferation of cyber technology and its development into many new forms over the last three decades has added a new dimension to cyber strategies, created new threats opportunities for cyber espionage and information warfare in cyberspace. The technological expansion of the Internet beyond computers and mobile phones into smart systems has created the threat of remote exploitation.

In 2016, a GCHQ-led National Cyber Security Centre (NCSC), and a Computer Emergency Response Team, were established to coordinate with international partners. In 2013, Cyber Reserve Unit was already in operation to recruit more hackers for the future war in cyberspace. In 2015, National Crime Agency and the National Cyber-crime Unit (NCCU) conducted operations against malware threats, while NCA and GCHQ launched a Specialist Joint Operation Cell (SJOC) in 2015 to improve response to cyber-crime. However, the same year, the Foreign and Commonwealth Office (FCO) admitted the existence of the Centre for Cyber Assessment (CCA).

In Britain, the police and the National Crime Agency, Intelligence, Home Office and the Defense Ministry in cooperation with GCHQ have tried to expand their efforts to identify and disrupt hostile cyber networks and their foreign sponsors. These efforts helped improve the state institutions system. As we read in newspapers and books, foreign espionage has also been a challenging issue in the UK during the last two decades. Espionage via Cyber Operations (CO) was more challenging, more discreet and faster than traditional espionage mechanisms.

Cyber terrorism is just as dangerous as biological and chemical attacks that deeply affect civilian life. This sort of threat requires a multi-tiered response. The United Kingdom, the US, and China operate through ECHELON, PRISM, TEMPORA, GHOSTHUNTER and GHOSTWOLF, MENWITH Hill and UPSTREAM, and invaded millions Internets, super computers, sites and state and private institutions across the globe. The Chinese PLA and American NSA are still fighting for important military and industrial data in Europe and Asia. All these spy networks deeply affected the day to day life of British citizens whose computers and privacy is not safe.

Cyber security and information technology development during the last decades evolved, and are now became part of our lives. As Britain is a digitalized society, for that reason the prosperity of the country depends on digital foundations. As the misuse of Internet prompted many law enforcement challenges, the UK and EU member states developed professional security measures to improve the watchdog system. The Internet expansion and its use by different hands generated a threat of remote exploitation to the whole technological infrastructure in the region. Terrorist and extremist networks continue to disrupt the institutional networks, and national critical infrastructure of the United Kingdom. Now, meeting these challenges require professional national security approach and counter-terrorism measures.

Cyber terrorism is also becoming a violent threat in Britain and Europe. Experts view it as a precarious threat to economic and financial institutions, and as a new threat to nuclear installations. For that reason it is an aggregate of number of factors. With an exponentially growing cyber threat to data, the US Foreign Intelligence Surveillance Authority (FISA) and the UK TEMPORA have introduced new measures and new surveillance systems to identify and disrupt foreign sponsor cyber terror networks. In Germany, Chancellor Angela Merkel reacted to the GCHQ and NSA spying campaign against the state institutions of the country in 2013. "Spying among friends" is unacceptable, she said.

The EU and Britain, like the US, are engaged in a broad range of data collection operations and are constantly seeking access to sensitive information from their rivals, especially Russia, China and Iran, but smaller countries, and even their allies, as well. And all of those countries, including Israel, are doing the same. For political reasons, research reports highlight Russian and Chinese cyber intelligence networks targeting the United States and Britain's industry and other installations. In 2014 and 2015, State Department and some of EU and UK state and private institutions came under attacks by these networks. Moreover, experts also spotlighted a new malware device used by these networks as APT28 to steal sensitive data from MAC devices, including backups and passwords.

In a different sphere of activity, in 2016 some harrowing incidents across the country caused panic when terrorists tried to attack public and government installations with chemical and biological weapons to create fear and uncertainty in London. Before these incidents, the Scotland Yard police recruited and deployed hundreds of highly armed commandos in cities and towns as part of a plan to beef up security, following a spate of deadly terrorist attacks in Europe. These officers were entrusted with the task of securing major landmarks across London. The force was equipped with massive machine guns, heavy-duty military-grade equipment and Kevlar body amour.

In view of this intensifying security environment in the country, Commissioner of Metropolitan Police, Sir Bernard Hogan-Howe announced a plan to put more force on ground, armed to respond to the revolving national security threats. Sir Hogan-Howe said that many terror-related attacks had been foiled due to the collaboration between the police, and intelligence agencies. Metropolitan Police is facing unprecedented difficulty in dealing with criminal gangs, serious organized crime, kidnapping, drug trafficking, illegal immigrants, terrorist networks, extremism and racism across the country, while some research reports highlighted the countrywide operation of foreign sponsored serious organized crime and human trafficking networks in conjunction with spy networks-challenging the authority of law enforcement agencies.

The performance of government prevent strategy has been very poor in the past. Law enforcement agencies were unable to infiltrate into the networks of foreign terrorist groups. Amidst terrorist attacks in Paris, Germany, and Brussels, the EU strategic vision and common security policy also failed to address the challenges of terrorism, sectarianism, home grown extremism and national security. For that reason intellectuals and scholars criticized the weak approach of the EU member states to national security and common strategy. As we read in newspapers and books, the current European societies face numerous challenges including radicalization, the lack of coordination among their policing institutions, and the inattention of governments to adopt effective security measures. Security experts suggest that a smooth and secure cross border intelligence information exchange between the law enforcement agencies of all EU member states can be very effective in fixing the windows of the professionalization of intelligence cooperation.

The issue of border checking is also facing challenges as watch lists are maintained poorly, and the lack of up-to-date information further exacerbated the problem. Guns and other firearms are still easily available in all EU states, which facilitate terrorists to carry out attacks on public places. However, notwithstanding its internal turmoil, Britain developed its own thesis and argued that the weak European counter-terror efforts and poor intelligence sharing cannot restore the confidence of the country. The UK Foreign Minister frankly remarked and said that the EU lacks effective intelligence mechanism. In an interview with the Financial Times, Hammond said: "Our intelligence agencies work seamlessly together. We don't talk about the different agencies in government—whether it is MI6, MI5, or GCHQ. We just talk about the single intelligence [output]. There are different legal structures, different powers, and often there are even turf wars, all of which reduce the operational effectiveness of [other countries' agencies] compared to ours".

Relations between Britain and the EU member states remain strained, while the country reviewed its law enforcement mechanism and intelligence strategies. In 2016, British government promulgated a new surveillance law which was a sign of deteriorating security, and law and order. On 17 January 2017, Prime Minister Theresa May's speech enraged the entire European Union. She was critical of the EU attitude towards Britain. "The UK cannot possibly remain within the EU single market, as staying in it would mean not leaving the EU at all," she said. EU leaders warned that the UK cannot be permitted to access the single market, which allows the free movement of goods, services and workers between its members, while at the same time restricting the free movement of people — and the PM has pledged to control EU migration. Mrs. May also indicated that the UK's relationship with the customs union — under which EU countries all impose the same tariff on goods imported from outside the EU but do not impose tariffs on each other's goods — would change. She said she did not want the country to be "bound" by the shared external tariffs. Instead, the UK would be "striking our own comprehensive trade agreements with other countries." Her London speech and her subsequent visit to World Economic Forum in Davos also raised several important questions regarding the UK's intelligence and security cooperation with the EU.

On 13 March 2017, The Independent published an article by expert Ben Chapman, reviewing the Prime Minister's stance on Brexit, the free market and free movement of people: "Theresa May confirmed months ago the UK will leave the EU's single market as she laid out her government's Brexit vision. In the same speech, the UK Prime Minister set out a list of her 'negotiating priorities' for the upcoming talks. Ms May had for months refused to confirm that she was taking the country out of the EU's single market and customs union and had also rejected the term 'hard Brexit.' But it is now clear the Brexit she is pursuing 'cannot mean membership of single market.' Restrictions on free movement of people appear to be an inevitable part of any deal and no country that is part of the single market currently implements immigration curbs. The European single market is the most ambitious part of the whole 'European project.' It aims to break down all barriers to trading across the 500 million-person area by ensuring the 'four freedoms' sacrosanct to Brussels policymakers: free movement of goods, services, capital and — most controversially — labor. As an EU member, the UK has signed up to each of those freedoms which, as Brussels has repeatedly made clear, are non-negotiable."

Mr. Eren Waitzman defended the Prime Minister on 20 January 2017:

> The European single market is an internal market which currently encompasses all 28 EU member states. A number of other European countries outside the EU also participate in the single market, such as Iceland, Liechtenstein and Norway, who are parties to the European Economic Area (EEA) agreement, and Switzerland, which has a number of bilateral agreements with the EU. The UK joined the then European Economic Community (EEC) in January 1973, with the single market as it exists today being established in 1992. The single market provides for the 'four freedoms' within the EU: the freedom of movement for goods, services, capital and people. In a speech on 17 January 2017, the Prime Minister, Theresa May, confirmed that the Government, in negotiating the UK's withdrawal from the EU, would seek a bespoke model for future UK–EU relations.

The Snowden revelations had already caused tension between the EU and UK governments. On 13 June 2013, the Washington Post and the Guardian published important stories about the information leaked by Edward Snowden, which exposed the US and UK secret data gathering mechanism through ECHELON, PRISM, UPSTREAM, MENWITH Hill, and TEMPORA. For years, experts and researchers were in tense struggle to find true information about this secret system, while human rights groups were actively seeking transparency about its operations, but policy makers in London often refused to provide information about the role of MENWITH Hill in national security. Recently, a top secret document obtained by Intercept offered good information about this system. Over the last ten years, NSA had been secretly running new spying system with names such as GHOSTHUNTER and GHOSTWOLF, which supported the UK and US military operations against al Qaeda in Afghanistan and Iraq. Moreover, another spy satellite was operating in 2009 from MENWITH Hill for intercepting communications. However, to identify Internet cafes across Middle East and Africa supporting US operations against terrorism in the region, GHOSTHUNTER was in full operation in 2009 that geo-located more than 5,000 Very Small Aperture Terminals (VSAT) as a satellite system used by governments in the region.

After these revelations, simply, the UK intelligence committee declared that the allegations that GCHQ had acted illegally by accessing the content of private communications via the PRISM program were "unfounded". In 2015, the ISC conducted inquiry into the capabilities of electronic intelligence in intrusive techniques. The Intelligence Committee concluded that the existing legal framework governing these capabilities was unnecessarily complicated, and recommended that it be replaced with a new Act of Parliament.

On 09 February 2016, in his Daily Dot article, Eric Geller noted the power mechanism of GCHQ in data collection: "GCHQ can collect "external" communications in bulk under a section 8(4) warrant. It can then search for and select communications to examine using a selector of an individual who is overseas, providing the Secretary of State has certified this as necessary for statutory purposes. If GCHQ wants to search for and select "external" communications to examine based on a selector of an individual in the UK, they must get additional authorization from a Secretary of State which names that person. The Secretary of State cannot issue section 8(1) or section 8(4) warrants unless they believe it is both necessary and proportionate".

In January 2016, Reprieve, an international human rights organization reported that members of the UK's Parliamentary intelligence watchdog would not be allowed access to all intelligence or defense information relating to the new British practice of targeted killing by drone. David Cameron was asked by Andrew Tyre (MP) that whether the Intelligence and Security Committee (ISC) would be allowed to examine the military aspect of the targeted killing program, and whether he would commit to the Committee's security-cleared members being able to see all the relevant intelligence. Reprieve reported.

Mr. Cameron, according to the Reprieve report, refused on both points, stating that the ISC's job was to examine intelligence, not military affairs, and that he could not give the commitment. Amidst these controversies, Prime Minister David Cameron visited Washington to further promote the UK's cyber skills. A select band of UK cyber-defense companies accompanying Cameron in this trip. Wall Street Journal reported Cameron's plan to ask the President face-to-face to criticize US tech companies such as Microsoft, Face book, Google and Apple who, post-Snowden, have started to encrypt their communications by default.

The British government quietly re-wrote the law to permit its electronic intelligence agency to continue with controversial surveillance practices. In a statement, Privacy International said: "The government has quietly ushered through legislation amending the anti-hacking laws to exempt GCHQ from prosecution. Privacy International and other parties were notified of these just hours prior to a hearing of their claim against GCHQ's illegal hacking operations in the Investigatory Powers Tribunal."

After the Snowden revelations in June 2013, a number of challenges to GCHQ's surveillance practices were initiated in the UK. In response to one of those applications, from Liberty and several other organizations, the court that oversees the GCHQ ruled against the UK intelligence services for the first time in its controversial 15 year history. In its two pages decision, Investigatory Powers Tribunal declared that, before December 2014 "the regime governing the soliciting, receiving, storing and transmitting by the UK authorities of private communications of individuals in the UK, which have been obtained by the US authorities" under the NSA's PRISM and UPSTREAM programs breached Articles 8 and 10 of the European Convention on Human Rights.

Some intellectual debates in the UK concluded that the UK, Germany, France, Poland and Netherlands intelligence agencies are professional and powerful, well-staffed, and efficient but others are shambolic or close to non-existent. Belgium's intelligence service was under-resourced and understaffed in 2016, with little cooperation between it and the myriad different police services. The Belgian Interior Minister warned about the attitude of Muslim extremists who danced after the deadly Brussels attacks. In an interview with a Belgian newspaper, Mr. Jan Jambon said he regretted that a "significant" proportion of the Muslim community had been "dancing" in the streets following the attacks on March 22 in which 32 innocent victims and three suicide bombers were killed, and over 300 people injured. "They threw stones and bottles at police and press during the arrest of Saleh Abdel Salam. That is the real problem. That migrants from the third or fourth generation turn openly against our society and have been willing to use violence or to justify it has to do with our policy," Mr. Jambon warned.

The Paris terrorist attacks in 2015, followed by the Copenhagen and Brussels terror attacks in 2016, changed the whole picture of the professionalization of intelligence cooperation within the EU. In all EU member states, thousands asylum seekers from South Asia, Afghanistan and the Arab world showing fake identity documents claimed asylum, but their real identity was not known. Their source of military training and source of terror finance come from the states where they live. The EU citizens who became radicalized fighting in Syria, Iraq and Afghanistan returned with new ideologies, perceptions and resolves.

Musa Khan Jalalzai
London
September 2017

CHAPTER 1. SECURING THE INSECURE STATES: LAW ENFORCEMENT, RADICALIZATION, EXTREMISM, AND JIHADISM IN EUROPE AND THE UNITED KINGDOM

Recent terrorist attacks in Manchester, London, Germany and France exposed the weakness of the EU's joint counter-terrorism strategy and intelligence sharing at the law enforcement level. Furthermore, intelligence agencies throughout the EU have been in deep crisis since the United Kingdom stepped backward due to its reservations and complaints about the attitude of EU member states. The EU intelligence agencies were unable to lead British policy makers through their illusory information due to the priorities of different stakeholders.

There are different perceptions of mechanisms, function and demonstration of intelligence in Europe, which make intelligence distinctive from the intelligence infrastructure of the US and Britain. The EU intelligence apparatuses lack reforms, coordination, and certain professional capabilities as it revolves around an inappropriate operational philosophy. The lack of coordination and cooperation at the law enforcement level is indicatives of their frustration and mutual mistrust. Ethnic and sectarian elements are also making things worse as they want to further their agenda of division rather than unity.

Lone wolf operations and the threat of radicalization of local citizens are growing in tandem with the problem of some dubious refugees. Ethnic, sectarian and political confrontations cause many problems that also affect the performance of intelligence operations. The Lisbon Treaty notes that the member states are in charge of intelligence agencies, but without good intelligence sharing, information collection and information processing, policy makers have no guidance to base their decisions on.

In 2016, terrorists carried out more than 142 attacks against eight European states. The United Kingdom and France reported 100 attacks while Italy, Spain, Greece, Germany, Belgium and Netherlands reported 66 attacks. Violent conflict in the EU member states, new hybrid threats and terrorist attacks strengthened the willingness in society to intensify European cooperation on foreign, security and defense levels. Cyber terrorism presents an increasing security threat. Cyber-attacks on states and critical infrastructures have long been a reality.

After the Paris, Brussels and Berlin terrorist attacks, the EU member states decided to establish a strong unified intelligence and security network to effectively defeat radicalization and extremism, but all dreams vanished due to their wariness. There are different priorities, resources and level of expertise within every state, every intelligence agency, and every bureaucratic set up, but intelligence sharing among as many as 28 member states is not an easy task as it seems. Stakeholder and private partners want their share, and modification. Policy makers and secret services face numerous legal, technical and political obstacles. Large states such as France, Germany, and the UK have established sizable counter-terrorism institutions with human resources to maintain sophisticated intelligence networks, but never tried to share classified intelligence information with other EU member states. This shortcoming caused misunderstanding and misgivings. In the meanwhile, terrorists started proliferating in Europe, armed and well-trained.

Given the limited cooperation on security issues, even after six decades of integration the EU remains a weak, fragile, and delicate project. And that is not likely to improve after Brexit.

A major concern related to the increasing radicalization of certain population segments in the EU member states is the phenomenon of "lone wolves" returning from Syria and Iraq. In 2016, it was estimated that more than 5,000 Europeans travelled to Iraq, Afghanistan and Syria. Foreign fighters have already carried out attacks on civilian and government installations in the EU. The Europol report indicated these elements belong to different ideologies and sects that justify the killing of non-Muslims. Some such lone wolf extremists have been arrested in several EU member states: in 2013, there were 216; in 2014, 395; and in 2015 there were 268.

Researcher Martina Elvira Salerno (2014) spotlighted some important terror-related incidents in Europe:

> In 2015, France suffered a number of jihadist terrorist attacks. On 7 January, two gunmen attacked the editorial staff of the French satirical magazine Charlie Hebdo in their office in Paris, killing twelve and wounding eight people. On 13 November, a series of attacks, perpetrated by three teams, were carried out in Paris in a football stadium, a theatre, cafés and restaurants. Overall 130 people were killed, including 89 at the Bataclan theatre. The Islamic State claimed responsibility for these acts, which clearly aimed to cause mass casualties. In addition to the attacks in France, on 14 February, a gunman attacked a free-speech debate in Copenhagen, Denmark. On 17 September, an Iraqi individual resident in Germany, classified by the authorities as a potentially dangerous Islamist extremist, attacked a female police officer with a knife on a Berlin street. On 6 December, a man was arrested by police after stabbing three people at a London Underground station. A witness claimed that the suspect screamed 'this is for Syria'. These events are some of the jihadist terrorist attacks which occurred in Europe in 2015. Given that the threat of jihadist terrorism 5 is widespread across Europe, it is necessary to understand what this expression actually means.[1]

Terrorist attacks in various EU member states prompted different law enforcement strategies, laws and countering mechanism that helped the intelligence and policing agencies to understand the basic motive behind the accelerating radicalization and violence in the continent. Notwithstanding all these efforts, responses and policing reforms, the EU citizen are still under threat from the lone wolves and radicalized elements, who justify the killing of non-Muslim in their transmogrified religious ideology. Specialist in European Affairs, Mr. Kristin Archick (February 27, 2017) highlighted historical and legal journey of the European Union:

> On November 1, 1993, the Treaty on European Union (also known as the Maastricht Treaty) went into effect, encompassing the EC and establishing the modern-day European Union. The EU was intended as a significant step on the path toward not only greater economic integration but also closer political cooperation.

---

[1] Terrorism in the EU: An overview of the current situation as reported by Europol, Martina Elvira Salerno, Giurisprudenza Penale Web 2016

The Maastricht Treaty contained provisions that resulted in the creation of the Eurozone, in which participants share a common currency, a common central bank (the European Central Bank, or ECB), and a common monetary policy (there is no common fiscal policy, however, and member states retain control over national spending and taxation, subject to certain conditions designed to maintain budgetary discipline).The Maastricht Treaty also set out a blueprint for greater coordination on foreign policy and internal security issues. Since the mid-1990s, EU member states have worked to forge a Common Foreign and Security Policy (CFSP), including a Common Security and Defense Policy (CSDP), and sought to establish common policies in the area of Justice and Home Affairs (JHA). In the late 1990s, the Schengen Agreement of 1985—which established the framework for eliminating border controls among participating states—became EU law. With the end of the Cold War, the EU pursued further enlargement. Austria, Finland, and Sweden joined in 1995. Enlargement to Central and Eastern Europe was an especially key priority viewed as fulfilling a historic pledge to further the integration of the continent by peaceful means and promote stability and prosperity throughout Europe. In 2004, eight formerly communist countries (the Czech Republic, Estonia, Hungary, Latvia, Lithuania, Poland, Slovakia, and Slovenia) acceded to the EU, along with Cyprus and Malta. Bulgaria and Romania joined in 2007. Croatia became the EU's newest member on July 1, 2013.[2]

However, the House of Lords also reviewed security cooperation between the UK and EU member states in its report on the future of UK–EU security and police cooperation, (16 December 2016):

> The UK currently enjoys what the Government has described as a "special status" in relation to EU cooperation on Justice and Home Affairs (JHA) matters. Specifically, it has negotiated the right to "opt in" to EU measures in this area, allowing the Government to decide, on a case-by-case basis, whether it is in the national interest to participate. When the UK does not choose to opt in, it is not bound by the EU measure in question. The practical implication of this is that cooperation on police and security matters between the UK and the EU is already limited to those measures that successive UK Governments have assessed to be in the national interest, rather than extending to the full spectrum of EU activity in those areas.[3]

---

[2] The European Union: Current Challenges and Future Prospects Specialist in European Affairs, Mr. Kristin Archick February 27, 2017, Congressional Research Service

[3] House of Lords-European Union Committee, 7th Report of Session 2016–17 HL Paper 77 Brexit: Future UK–EU security and police cooperation, 16 December 2016.

As mentioned earlier, the security crisis in the EU still causes trouble for traders, investors and law enforcement authorities. Extremists in various European states have received terrorist training in Pakistan, Afghanistan, Iraq and Syria, and receive huge funds from Qatar and Saudi Arabia. Recent reports of EU research institutions indicate that the Saudi funding of Islamic terrorist groups in Britain and EU member states enraged the entire region.

In the 1990s and 2000s, member states struggled to address terror-related issues and significant changes in Europe's security environment. The heightened terrorism threat also poses risks to the Schengen area of free movement.

Political and geographical turmoil in Easter European states has made the unity of the continent doubtful. The states of the Western Balkans such as Albania, Bosnia and Herzegovina, Kosovo, Macedonia, Montenegro, and Serbia are boiling in their own ovens. Ethnically and culturally, some of these are naturally more closely related to Russia, and China has been a beneficial partner to them over the past decades as well. This makes it difficult for the EU to draw them in and treat them as long-term partners. Analyst Marko Prelec (2017) noted some aspects of insecurity in the region:

> The ability of the European Union (EU) to fix problems in the Balkans is hamstrung when the same troubles persist within its own borders, sometimes in more acute form. Take erosion of democratic norms: Hungary over the past decade has slid from 2.14 to 3.54 on Freedom House's "Nations in Transit" democracy score (lower is better). Poland's decline is more recent but equally steep. Croatia is also backsliding. Almost all the Western Balkan states are declining, too, but more slowly. The familiar image of the Balkans is of a region with lots of minority problems: small groups that are oppressed or want to break away. Today, though, the most bitter and dangerous conflicts in most of the states there are between parties that appeal mostly or exclusively to the majority ethnic community. Minorities are bystanders, pulled in against their wishes.[4]

The struggle against radicalization and extremism in EU is on the core of the union's security and justice areas. The EU have taken several important security and legal measures to address the issue of lone wolves and radicalized elements returning from Syria. All member states jointly established a security network by a continuous

---

[4] Europe and Central Asia, 28 APRIL 2017, New Balkan Turbulence Challenges Europe, Marko Prelec

harmonized approach in the area of intelligence and law enforcement cooperation. White Paper (2017) of the European Union highlighted the political and economic crisis of member states:

> The EU is now the place where Europeans can enjoy a unique diversity of culture, ideas and traditions in a Union covering four million square kilometers. It is where they have forged life-long bonds with other Europeans and can travel, study and work across national borders without changing currency. It is where the rule of law has replaced the rule of the iron fist. It is where equality is not just spoken about but continues to be fought for. Despite this, many Europeans consider the Union as either too distant or too interfering in their day-to-day lives. Others question its added-value and ask how Europe improves their standard of living. And for too many, the EU fell short of their expectations as it struggled with its worst financial, economic and social crisis in post-war history. Europe's challenges show no sign of abating. Our economy is recovering from the global financial crisis but this is still not felt evenly enough. Parts of our neighborhood are destabilized, resulting in the largest refugee crisis since the Second World War. Terrorist attacks have struck at the heart of our cities.[5]

Today's advanced state machine includes physical infrastructures, such as energy, air and maritime transport, railways, water-supply, telecommunication networks, and manufacturing industries. The smooth and continuous functioning of these elements is essential for the social and economic development of a state. These components are also under threat from the home-grown radicalized elements who receive training from Pakistan, Afghanistan, Syria and Iraq. They are being funded by the Saudi and Qatar governments. On 07 July 2017, the Guardian reported four Arab states boycotted against Qatar and said that Doha's refusal of their demands was proof of its links to terrorist groups, and that they would enact new measures against it. Saudi Arabia, the United Arab Emirates, Egypt and Bahrain released a joint statement carried by their state media said their initial list of 13 demands was now void and pledging new political, economic and legal steps against Qatar. The Newspaper reported.[6] In a recent

---

[5] White Paper on the Future of Europe: Reflections and scenarios for the EU27 by 2025, European Commission

[6] On 07 July 2017, The Guardian reported four Arab states boycotted against Qatar and said that Doha's refusal of their demands was proof of its links to terrorist groups and that they would enact new measures against it.

research report of Henry Jackson Society (July 2017), Tom Wilson highlighted the funding of Islamic extremism in the UK:

> In June 2017 the UK government pledged to establish a commission for countering extremism. The challenge of foreign funded Islamist extremism is one area that could be prioritized by this new body. There is a clear lack of publicly available information on this subject and the Home Office has said that the research being carried out by the Extremism Analysis Unit may never be published. As such, an open and public inquiry into the funding of extremism from overseas would represent an important step toward formulating policy to address this problem. While Britain may not choose to introduce legislation for blocking foreign funding, measures might be considered that would oblige institutions to show more transparency on certain kinds funding from abroad. Following the recent Islamist terror attacks in Manchester and London, and a wave of terrorism in continental Europe, the threat level in the UK remains at Severe, meaning further attacks are highly likely. As of 2015 the national counter-terrorism strategy has placed increased emphasis on addressing the role that non-violent Islamist extremism and extremist ideology plays in ultimately leading some individuals to commit acts of violence. In the Queen's Speech of June 2017, the government announced that as part of this effort it would establish a Commission for Countering Extremism.[7]

In July 2017, the G20 nations in Germany exchanged opinions on the future of EU and NATO, and discussed joint action plan for fighting extremism, radicalization and terrorism. On 27 June 2017, BBC published report on the Brexit and negotiation between Britain and the EU member states to find a reasonable solution to the persisting crisis. Prime Minister Theresa May offered that all EU nationals lawfully resident in the UK for at least five years will be able to apply for "settled status" and be able to bring over spouses and children. But EU member states said they were not satisfy with this offer, Britain needs to do more. The key points of the Prime Minister Proposals and offer are:

1. Those granted settled status will be able to live, work, study and claim benefits just as they can now
2. The cut-off date for eligibility is undecided but will be between 29 March 2017 and 29 March 2019

---

[7] Foreign Funded Islamist Extremism in the UK, Centre for the Response to Radicalization and Terrorism, Research Paper No. 9, Tom Wilson, the Henry Jackson Society, July 2017.

3. Family members of EU citizens living abroad will be able to return and apply for settled status
4. EU nationals in the UK for less than five years at the specified date will be able to continue living and working in the UK
5. Once resident for five years, they can apply for settled status
6. Those arriving after the cut-off point will be able to stay temporarily
7. But there should be "no expectation" they will be granted permanent residence
8. A period of "blanket residence permission" may apply to give officials time to process applications to stay in the UK
9. The Home Office will no longer require evidence that EU citizens who weren't working held "comprehensive sickness insurance.[8]

Recent terror attacks in France and UK once again pinpointed the issue of security cooperation among EU member states. Some states suggested the creation of a European Intelligence Agency, while some rejected the idea and said who will control it and how it will operate. Radicalization and terrorism are major issue, but a unified security approach is also needed. This will mean countries will seek renewed forms of cooperation, but to think of a unified intelligence service is a totally different issue. The threat of lone wolves returning from Syria and Iraq is severe. They attacked France in 2015 and London in 2017. In January 2017, European Parliament's Policy Department for Citizens Rights and Constitutional Affairs published a comprehensive report on its counter terrorism policy, which highlighted the EU efforts in the field of intelligence and countering radicalization and extremism:

> On the EU level, some interesting developments have occurred in recent years. In parallel to the evolution of Europol's European Counter Terrorism Centre (ECTC), the Counter Terrorism Group (CTG) has been strengthened in 2016 by introducing a common platform for the exchange of information between Member States' security services, accompanied by secure infrastructure for timely and safe communication. According to the Commission, it is now urgent to reinforce the two tracks of the ECTC and the CTG, keeping them separate but linking the two communities, which would add up to an effective counter-terrorism cooperation framework in Europe, without the need for new structures. The Commission therefore calls

---

[8] Brexit: All you need to know about the UK leaving the EU By Alex Hunt & Brian Wheeler BBC News, 27 June 2017

upon the Member States to "facilitate an information exchange hub based on the interaction between the law enforcement community and the intelligence community, within the framework of the CTG and the ECTC, in accordance with relevant EU and national rules and arrangements." However, it is a vast leap between interaction between the two communities and an 'information exchange hub.[9]

Currently, as the process of Brexit begins, the British Prime Minister warned about the reduced security cooperation if her country is not "treated fairly." After this warning, EU member states decided to improve cooperation on information sharing at the law enforcement level — but it didn't happen. And terrorists attacked Manchester and London and killed innocent civilians. Netherlands, Germany, France, Slovakia, Romania, Spain, Belgium, and Bulgaria did adopt security sector reforms, and implemented firearms directives. Britain and the EU member states have been engaged in an intense debate over the fate of EU immigration as the graph of crime culminated, and an increasing number of incidents of terrorism, serious organized crime, and hate crime challenged the efforts of law enforcement agencies to tackle the deteriorating security situation in the region since 2014.

In 1993, cooperation on law enforcement with EU becomes formal part of EU activity with the entry into force of the Treaty of Maastricht. In 1985, five states signed the Schengen agreement that provided for the gradual abolition of internal border controls and a common visa policy. In 1999 the treaty of Amsterdam became into force that created the concept of an Area of Freedom Security and Justice (AFSJ). In 2009, the Lisbon treaty came into force that merged police and judicial cooperation in criminal matters into the main EU structures for cooperation on Justice and Home Affairs. On law enforcement level, the UK shared data with the EU law enforcement authorities.

On 10 November 2016, the Information Commissioner of the United Kingdom in his response to the House of Common Justice Committee consultation on the implication of Brexit for the justice system, and elucidated his responsibilities for promoting and enforcing the Data Protection Act 1998 (DPA) and the Freedom of Information Act 2000 (FOIA), the Environmental Information

---

[9] In January 2017, European Parliament's Policy Department for Citizens' Rights and Constitutional Affairs published a comprehensive report on its counter terrorism policy, which highlighted the EU efforts in the field of intelligence and countering radicalization and extremism

Regulations (EIR) and the Privacy and Electronic Communications Regulations 2003, as amended (PECR). The commissioner in his detailed response also illuminated the change in data protection law on EU level, and said that the case for continued participation in Europol, Eurojust, the European Arrest Warrant, the European Criminal Records Information System (ECRIS) the Prum package and other cross-border law-enforcement measures will be made by others but he will continue to make the case for a continued high standard of data protection safeguards if the UK opts out of these regimes. The Commissioner explained his position on the arrangement of data sharing with Europol and Eurojust:

> The Commissioner is clear that any separate bilateral agreements entered into must not dip below current UK and internationally recognized standards. It may well be the case that to enter into a bilateral arrangement to share data with bodies such as Europol or Eurojust, the UK would have to demonstrate essential equivalence in meeting the data protection safeguards established within those bodies. At a more general level, the UK's departure from the European Union comes at the very time when EU level data protection law is changing and this will take effect before the UK has left. At present, organizations processing data for law enforcement and justice purposes have to comply with the requirements of the DPA and, in respect of the processing of personal data for cross-border law enforcement purposes, to Part 4 of The Criminal Justice and Data Protection (Protocol No. 36) Regulations 2014 (the '2014 Regulations'). The DPA governs all aspects of the processing of personal data for domestic law enforcement purposes, as well as the processing of personal data by law enforcement agencies which is not for law enforcement purposes (for example for their own internal record-keeping, administration, personnel records, etc.). The 2014 Regulations apply in circumstances outside the reach of the DPA, for example when co-operating with an overseas law enforcement agency, but the provisions are broadly consistent with the DPA.[10]

The UK Information Commissioner also noted that the present turmoil within the EU and its soured relationship with the UK government after the Brexit referendum in 2016 may cause risk in terms of protecting the personal data of UK citizens. Notably,

---

[10] The Information Commissioner's response to the House of Commons Justice Committee consultation on the implications of Brexit for the justice system, 10 November 2016

The Government has still to make clear the implementation arrangements for the Law Enforcement Directive and which legislative vehicle will cover the processing of personal data for law enforcement purposes. Uncertainty around the UK's future relationship with the European Union has compounded this uncertainty amongst those organizations likely to be affected. The potential reach of this legislation will be wide covering law enforcement agencies, public sector bodies with criminal prosecution functions, the prison service, the criminal court system and potentially other organizations which will fall within scope. The Commissioner is concerned that there will be a fragmented legislative regime. From a regulatory perspective this will be challenging and the complexities of this brings with it risks in terms of protecting the processing of the personal data of UK citizens. It is important that in term of protecting the processing of the personal data of UK citizens.[11]

On 14 November 2016, the UK Home Office announced its intention to remain a full member of Europol, an EU-wide law enforcement agency, until Britain's formal exit from the union. This was one the first major opt-in/out decisions taken by Theresa May's Government since the referendum, and it reflected warnings that the UK risked losing access to vital intelligence. Europol was created in 1998 to bring together criminal intelligence and share information between police and security forces across the EU.

British citizens voted to leave the EU in 2016 because the costs appeared to outweigh the benefits in the last few years. Intelligence sharing and the attitude of the member states towards Britain were disappointing. The EU had experienced numerous incidents of violence and terrorism, and their weak security approach and complicated intelligence infrastructure were shown to be in adequate to meet these new challenges.

The United Kingdom is facing numerous political, social and economic challenges since the vote on Brexit in June 2016. Internal political turmoil and a wide-ranging debate between the opposition and the ruling coalition have accompanied the triggering of Article 50.

Professor Edward Burke in his recent research paper also argued that the Brexit vote has embroiled Britain in a new crisis relating to Northern Ireland:

Brexit has also shaken the foundations of the peace process in Northern Ireland. The majority of Ulster's voters opposed Brexit,

---

[11] Ibid.

and Irish nationalists in the province believe that the constitutional changes it requires will reverse many of the gains of the Good Friday Agreement. In the coming Brexit negotiations, London should acknowledge Northern Ireland's unique relationship with the EU. A distinctive EU status for Northern Ireland, committing London and the 27 to maintaining many of the EU's structural and Ulster-specific programmes would help to limit the fallout from the UK's exit. In the event that the EU and the UK fail to agree quickly on a comprehensive free trade agreement, Brussels could work with London to create a specific regime for Irish and Northern Irish goods and services (including and beyond the exposed agri-food sector), exempting them from tariffs and most customs checks if they remain on the island of Ireland. Of all the nations and regions of the UK, Northern Ireland has the most compelling case to establish a separate, privileged relationship with the EU in the post-Brexit era.[12]

During the last two decades, police in the UK and the EU faced a daunting set of challenges. Pattern of crime changed, terrorists adopted new tactics, fear in society grew, and citizens were alienated from the state by illegal mass surveillance. British and EU politicians never realized how sensitive the region was to this the deteriorating law and order. Terrorists have a free ride. Successive governments established dozens of different policing research and intelligence units but the result has chiefly been confusion.

The London, Manchester and Paris terrorist attacks shattered all dreams of peace and stability and demonstrated that the police agencies had failed to counter radical groups. They recruit young men and women, send them to Syrian and Iraq for jihad, and then use them inside the UK and EU for terrorist attacks.

Prime Minister Theresa May noted that the fight against ISIS has moved "from the battlefield to the Internet." And she added that she would work with leaders and Internet technology companies to "stop the spread of hateful extremist ideology on social media."

At the same time, police officers in London continue to leave their posts due to their low salary and difficult work environment. A grim picture, taken altogether.

---

[12] Ulster's fight, Ulster's rights?: Brexit, Northern Ireland and the threat to British-Irish relations, Edward Burke, July 2017, Centre for European Reforms.

Chapter 2. UK Law Enforcement and the Fight Against Terrorism and Radicalization

In this chapter, I wish to highlight some aspects of the UK law enforcement agencies and their role in maintaining peace and security. At the outset, I need to discuss the evolution of the UK police force. The UK police and law enforcement agencies have in recent years gained experience in fighting terrorism and radicalization; let's look at where they began.

The origin of the police in Britain lies in early tribal history. In the past, community police were divided into groups of ten, called tithing. This system was established in 17th and 18th centuries.[13] Officers working under this system were in contact with their communities and acted like watchmen to maintain order. This traditional policing system was introduced for the first time by an Afghan king, Farid Khan (Sher Shah Suri) (1486–1545), who established the empire of North India. In this system (Watch-Men System), every village, community, city, and town had its own watch-men.[14]

Young people were recruited to patrol streets and towns and ensure the protection of communities. Community leaders were receiving fixed funds from the King to pay the salaries of the officers of their private policing organizations. King Farid Khan was a brilliant Afghan administrator as well as a strong military commander who reorganized his empire and made it strong, secure and prosperous. His

[13] Encyclopedia of Crime and Justice, the Gale Group Inc 2002 http://www.encyclopedia.com/law/legal-and-political-magazines/police-history
[14] Schimmel, Annemarie, Burzine K. Waghmar, 2004. *The Empire of the Great Mughals: History, Arts and Culture*, Reaction Books.

policing, postal, and revenue systems are still in place in Afghanistan, India and Pakistan. King Sher Shah remodeled the police system, made village headmen responsible for the maintenance of peace in their respective areas and prevented crimes like drinking and adultery through Muhtasibs (Ombudsmen). He maintained a strong standing army and an efficient intelligence system. A man with a strong sense of justice, the sultan was the highest court of appeal, both for civil and criminal cases. Next to him was the Qazi-ul-Quzzat (Chief Justice). In the Parganas the Qazi (Judge) administered criminal cases while the Amin looked after the civil ones. Panchayets (Informal Justice) decided the civil cases of the Hindus.

He instructed the revenue officials to show leniency at the time of assessment and to be strict at the time of collection of revenues. The rights of the tenants were duly recognized and the liabilities of each were clearly defined in the kabuliyat (deed of agreement), which the State took from him, and the patta (title-deed), which it gave him in return.

Law enforcement and policing systems in Britain during the 1700s were not administered on the national level; instead the system was being run by local communities. For 239 years (1674–1913), many changes occurred in the British policing system, while the old watch-men system was replaced by a salaried system of modern policing.[15]

In 1730 and later on, the policing system was improved and a specific amount was fixed to hire a watch man or constable dedicated to working for the protection of communities day and night. In London, Magistrates established rotation offices to encourage victims to report crime and share information about criminals with local police station.[16] In 1737, an act of policing was introduced to regulate the night policing system, and from 1674 to 1829, crime victims were able to identify criminals. With the introduction of this act, all irregular and self-styled forces and private armies were amalgamated in one strong and organized police force.[17]

In the 18th and 19th centuries, with the expansion of London's geographical boundaries, the issue of law and order management became greater. The modern police system in Britain was introduced

---

[15] The Proceeding of the Old Bailey, London's Central Criminal Court, 1674-1913, https://www.oldbaileyonline.org/static/Proceedings.jsp
[16] Ibid.
[17] Ibid.

by Sir Robert Peel (1829). He was an expert in policing and security, and worked as a Chief Secretary from 1812 to 1816, and as a Home Secretary from 1822 to 1830. During this period, he established the preservation force of peace.[18] In 1839, a separate police force was established for the city of London to ensure the safety and security of citizens.

He was the first Home Secretary in Britain who passed the Police Act from parliament, and established Metropolitan Police force in London. He defined the basic duty and function of the UK police, its relationship with community, the need for trust, and the test of its efficiency. The basic mission of the police was to prevent crime, and to maintain public respect and public cooperation. The police forces, according to his principles, needed to preserve public favor and protect lives. The police was responsible to restore order by physical force, when necessary. Finally, Sir Robert Peel suggested that the test of police efficiency was the absence of crime.

On 29 September 1829, Sir Robert Peel appointed Col. Sir Charles Rowan and Barrister Richard Mayne to lead the force and make it more effective. They formed a force of 895 selected constables, 88 sergeants, 20 inspectors, and 8 superintendents to lead the policing system, and make secure the lives of Londoners.[19]

The beginning was difficult due to the rapid increase in crime. Sir Peel introduced a reform bill in Parliament where he also highlighted to establish a unified force to effectively control crime and maintain order without the help of armed forces. His act became law in July 1829, and at the end of September that year, constables started patrolling the streets of London, commanding by two commissioners who were answerable to the Home Secretary.[20]

On 28 June 1830, due to the lack of understanding and knowledge of the policing culture in the city, first police constable Mr. Joseph Grantham was killed. In 1839, the Bow Street Runners, the Foot and Horse Patrol and other forces joined the Metropolitan police to make the force stronger.

In 1842, a new intelligence branch was formed to investigate crime. In 1878, the intelligence branch was named as Criminal Investigation

---

[18] International Centre for the History of Crime, Policing, Justice, Origins of the Metropolitan Police, www.open.ac.uk/Arts/history-from-police-archives/Met6Kt/MetHistory/mhFormMetPol.html
[19] Ibid.
[20] Ibid.

Department (CID). By 1900, more than 16,000 police officers were recruited and organized into 21 divisions. In 1912, special constables were reorganized as a modern force, while in 1934, it was named Metropolitan Special Constabulary.[21] In 1931, Mr. Hugh Trenchard was named police commissioner, and on 03 September 1939, while Britain joined the war, the strength of the police was barely 18,428. In 1950 and 1960, London was subject to demonstrations, and in 1965, Special Patrol Group (SPG) was formed to tackle crime and other law and order issues. In 1981, Lord Scarman reported racial discrimination cases within the police department, and the issue was spotlighted again in the 1999 Macpherson Report.[22]

A Central aspect of the UK model of policing is the principle of policing by consent, effectiveness, and cooperation with communities. The state is responsible to protect its citizens. Police has special power in society to tackle crime and law and order challenges. Public expectations from the police are their safety and security. The problems of communities' security and safety are biggest challenges of the police in a multicultural society where prevailing criminal cultures of Asia and Africa further challenged the writ of government. Since the 9/11, the UK police have been central to managing law and order, but with the arrival of hundreds of thousands of criminals from across the globe, police and its intelligence units have failed to counter their networks.[23]

The police operate under different social and political pressures with the changing times, and they face different cultures of crime. In 1992–1993, government began examining various aspects of policing in the UK and initiated three inquiries: the Royal Commission on Criminal Justice (RCCJ), the Sheehy Inquiry (SI) into Police Responsibilities, and White Paper of Home Secretary on Police Reforms (WPHSPR). These three inquiries deeply studied policing crisis and recommended radical changes in the structure of policing and its operational mechanism. Notwithstanding, these and other efforts to make the policing in Britain effective failed.[24]

---

[21] Official History of Metropolitan Police, http://content.met.police.uk/Site/history

[22] Ibid.

[23] Sir Robert Peel's principles of law enforcement, 1829

[24] The role and responsibilities of the police: Report of an independent inquiry established by the police foundation and the policy studies institute, 1996, and also, www.parliament.uk, https://www.publications.parliament.uk/pa/ld199596/ldhansrd/vo960501/text/60501-03.htm

An increasing role of private security agencies has been controversial. They also have influenced policing reform and the policy-making process. Tom Winsor was asked by the government to prepare a police reform package but his proposed reforms faced political and legal challenges. His shakeup of pay, conditions and recruitment policy was criticized by several policing agencies and their private partners. Professional and skilled police officers were discontented and started leaving their posts.

It was even proposed to integrate the Police Service of Scotland, Scottish Crime and Drug Enforcement Agency (SSCDEA) into a single service.[25]

Many issues remain unsolved, and many new questions arose after the Brexit referendum. Mistrust between the police and the public has been exacerbated. The UK introduced the strongest surveillance systems to tackle crime issues, but in the case of terrorism and radicalization, its surveillance system, TEMPORA, failed. In 2016, the London police commissioner warned that law enforcement agencies had lost the trust of communities after the revelations by Edward Snowden.[26]

The UK police have been fighting target killers, professional criminals, EU trained burglars, and terrorist and espionage networks for the last two decades, but no improvement occurred in the lives of citizens. Individuals and businesses are being targeted by the day. Law enforcement has been unable to satisfy communities due to the evolving nature of criminal networks. The police force lives in the past and criminal networks operate with modern tactics.

Recent developments in EU member states have presented new challenges to law enforcement as criminal mafia groups can easily pass from one state to another state, where they operate in different ways. Wanted criminals, sexual offenders, murderers, drug smugglers, child abusers, and spies are free to travel across Europe and establish networks.

In Scotland, local policing receives support from various quarters and communities to jointly work against organized criminal networks and focus on four objectives, the "4 D's":

1. Divert people from becoming criminals

---

[25] Ibid.
[26] *The Crisis of Britain's National Surveillance State: Law Enforcement, Surveillance and Intelligence War in Cyberspace*, Musa Khan Jalalzai, Algora Publishing, 2014

---

2. Deter serious organized groups
3. Detect and prosecute those involved in serious organized crime
4. Disrupt serious organized networks.[27]

Recently, print and electronic media reported on the conduct of the police, and its relationship with communities. Independent Police Complaints Commission (IPCC) has so far registered thousands of complaints against the behaviors of police officers. In view of these developments, government introduced the Policing and Crime Act 2017 to address issues like policing, discipline, inspection, operation and biometric system. On 2 March 2017, ITV reported national crisis of policing in Britain as more than 67,000 suspects still needed to be placed on police national computer. Large numbers of crime were written off, and insufficient action was taken in too many cases; victims were letdown and treated by abusive ways. More than 2,700 sex offenders were not assessed properly.[28]

Research reports of London-based think tanks raised important questions about the performance of state institutions and their mode of operation. Corruption, racism and discrimination left an ugly blot on the UK's multicultural face, while Scotland Yard and the Home Office were in hot water as their forces failed to demonstrate in a professional way. After every six months, government announces new security and immigration measures, which is indicative of its frustration and anxiety to control the prevailing environment of fear and discontent. However, government has lost its destiny and is now looking for a light to come out of this social quagmire.[29]

The Police Watchdog reports warned that the police is stuck in the past, using outdated methods to deal with modern, organized criminal networks across the country. Notwithstanding their access to modern technology, which enables them to act professionally, police officers lack proper skills, training and education? In the Rotherham child abuse case, the police Chief admitted failure: "This is a hideous crime. I am deeply embarrassed. I can say with honesty I had no idea of the scale and scope of this." However, the Home Affairs

---

[27] Glasgow Council 11 March 2016
[28] On 2 March 2017, ITV reported national crisis of policing in Britain as more than 67,000 suspects still needed to be placed on police national computer.
[29] Law Enforcement in the United States, James A. Conser, Rebecca Paynich, Terry Gingerich, Terry E. Gingerich, Jones & Bartlett Publishers, 21 Oct 2011

Select Committee also criticized the former chief constable on how his ignorance over these activities was "totally unconvincing".[30]

The growing numbers of terror-related incidents in EU and the United Kingdom prompted several law enforcement and intelligence reforms to design new strategies. After the Brexit referendum, the surge of racism and discrimination cases overwhelmed the UK police while the National Police Chiefs Council reported 57 percent rise in hate crime compared to 2015. On 02 July 2016, NPCC reported 6000 hate crimes, while discrimination and physical attacks in public places and buses caused deep concern for the local communities across the country. Though London is the birthplace of modern police force, and the idea of Sir Robert Peel (1829) to define an ethical police force, but residents of the city are in trouble to manage their daily lives.[31]

On 07 July 2017, TR News reported London witnessed up to three acid attacks every week. The report from the London based radio station comes after aspiring model and business student Resham Khan was attacked last month while sitting in her car with her cousin Jameel Muhktar. The recent acid attacks in the UK have enraged all minorities' communities. In East London acid attack on two Muslim cousins in London was treated as hate crime. Metropolitan police said new evidence came to light about attack in which Jameel Muhktar and Resham Khan suffered severe burns. The police named John Tomlin, 24, who frequents Canning Town, east London, as the suspected attacker and warned people to stay away if they see him. Jameel Muhktar and Resham Khan were attacked while sitting in a car at traffic lights in Beckton on the morning of 21 June while out celebrating Khan's 21st birthday. Mukhtar said that when a man knocked on the car window, at around 9.15am on 21 June, and sprayed the substance, he thought it was a practical joke. But he then noticed that his cousin was burning, and started to feel his clothes and trainers melting on to his body. A study carried out at a regional burns unit in Essex found only nine out of 21 victims pursued criminal charges against their attackers. During the last six years, more than 1,500 Acid Attacks Hit London and its outskirts. According to the daily Caller reported Jaf Shah told Guardian that there was a fairly large probability that a high percentage of the incidents are male-on-male attacks and most likely to be gang-related.

---

[30] *Daily Times*, 07 April, 2015
[31] Ibid.

The threat from international terrorism continues to evolve. Against this backdrop, British National Crime Agency (NCA) carried out several successful operations, breaking up criminal networks and re-establishing the rule of law where "No Go" areas were being maintained be smugglers and criminals. National Crime agency in its annual plan for 2016–17 (NCA Annual Plan 2016-17) outlined its operational mechanism and countering serious crime strategy: "Using the National Control Strategy, the National Strategic Tasking and Coordination Group (NSTCG) allocated threats and cross-cutting issues to multiagency Strategic Governance Group (SGGs). The SGGs, chaired by NCA Directors and Specialist Threat Group where necessary, produce Strategic Action Plan to describe the activity to be undertaken by the NCA and its partners to mitigate the threats and risks. Each Strategic Action Plan aligns with the Government's Serious and Organized Strategy, outlining activity against each of the 4Ps (Pursue, Prevent, Protect, and Prepare). A tasking and coordination cycle coordinated the national law enforcement responses to threats and risks, and ensures that operational resources are used to maximum impact".[32]

The performance of police service in Northern Ireland was reviewed by government through different accountability structures including the Police Ombudsman for Northern Ireland Policing Board (PONIPB), but no effective improvement occurred in community policing. The New Irish Republican Army (New IRA) continues to challenge the authority of the local government, and create fear in community. The New IRA is the restructure of old PIRA that wants to unify Ireland and Northern Ireland. In 2016, Chief of the UK Security Service (MI5), Andrew Parker warned that terrorist threat persists in Northern Ireland. The Guardian reported the statement of the paramilitary organization to mark the 100th anniversary of the Easter Rising against British rule in Ireland. The organization claimed that: "a century on and the IRA armed actions against Britain and her agents are [as] legitimate as they were in 1916". In their 2016 Easter statement, the New IRA said: "As we look to the future Britain is stuck in their colonial past. While their occupation, the accompanying denial of national self-determination and partition

---

[32] National Crime Agency *Annual Report*, 2016-17

remain the IRA will continue to target any and all of those who assist in those injustices."[33]

On 11 March 2015, BBC reported MI5 raised the alert level across Britain for a Northern Irish terrorist attack from "moderate to substantial".[34] Former Home Secretary, Theresa May said the MI5 alert reflects the persisting threat from dissident republican activity.

Cyber-crime is another challenge faced by police forces across the country and is considered a major threat to the UK security.[35]

The police forces are responsible to protect public and tackle terror-related incidents. There have been complaints that police does not respond to the grievances of minority communities. The issue of racism in the police department is mater of deep concern which prompted strained relationship between the police and communities. Experts suggested that the police operations and performance must be carried out in conjunction with communities in order to help them recognize diversity. In February 2015, the Independent newspaper reported the failure of Essex Police to investigate 30 child abuse cases. Vulnerable children were left at the mercy of child sex offenders after a police unit delayed the arrests of suspects during more than three years of systemic failure, the newspaper reported. On November 27, 2014, Her Majesty's Inspectorate of Constabulary (HMIC) published a report that criticized the police force for its inability to demonstrate skillfully.[36]

On March 9, 2015, BBC reported the police approach to law enforcement as peculiar, which typically involved waiting until a crime committed and then attempted to tackle it and arrest the criminal. This kind of approach no longer works as professional criminal gangs from Asia and Europe have adopted new strategies and technologies. The performance of the National Crime Agency (NCA) is also in question as the parameters of drug trafficking, human trafficking and fake currency trade have expanded.[37]

From borough-councils to police and NHS, all state and government institution are failing to deliver properly. The threat of institutional corruption still needs to be recognized. In the National Security

---

[33] *The Guardian*, 29 March 2016
[34] *BBC* 11 March 2015
[35] On March 9, 2015, BBC reported that Dal Babu, a former chief superintendent London police, said that many Muslims did not trust the prevention strategy.
[36] Ibid.
[37] The UK National Security Strategy, 14 December 2015

Strategy (NSS) of 2010, the word corruption is not mentioned until page 13. However, the Strategic Defense and Security Review (SDSR) 2010, which fleshes out some aspects and the NSS's implementation strategies, do not mention corruption at all. This indicates that corruption is not yet seen as relevant to all aspects of national security. This is a serious mistake that directly affects the development of an integrated strategy for reducing the risk of looming security threats.[38]

Hate crimes, motivated jihadism and the scourge of Islam-phobia have significantly intensified in London. Faith-related attacks have increased and Muslim students are suffering backlash and abuse in schools. Recently, The Independent reported that a teenage Muslim student at a school in Oxford shire was slapped and called a "terrorist". Members of the teachers union told the newspaper that there was an increase in Islam phobic incidents with the 400,000 Muslim students in schools increasingly likely to be jeered at as "terrorists", "pedophiles" or "immigrants". However, anti-Semitic incidents too reached a high level with record damage to property, abuse and threats. A Jewish NGO recorded more than 1,168 incidents in 2014. The home secretary termed the figure "deeply concerning". Criminal money continues to be channeled through UK banks to terrorists.[39]

Every day, the threat of terrorism and violent extremism is growing, which makes the police overactive. Racism has affected the law enforcement efforts. Racial inequality in the workplace has also worsened. The Macpherson Enquiry Report asserted that institutional racism brought a bad name to the UK. There are some pieces of legislation that remain ineffective. The government has placed terrorism as the top threat to the country but response to it has been unsatisfactory over the years. The police needs to improve its performance and reduce cost. Our policing must evolve along with the social make up of communities, inequalities and divisions. We need to create a police force that is professional, and accountable.[40]

Cyber terrorists and their challenging operations are more irksome as they continue to attack different institution by the day. The National Crime Cyber Unit (NCCU) leads the UK's response

---

[38] *The Independent*, 23 January 2015, and BBC 11 March 2015
[39] Carnegie Europe, 18 February 2015, and the Independent February 2015
[40] National Cyber Crime Unit, http://www.nationalcrimeagency.gov.uk/about-us/what-we-do/national-cyber-crime-unit, Daily Times, 18 November 2014

to cyber-crime, supports partners with specialist capabilities and coordinates the national response to the most serious of cyber threats:

> The NCCU is pursuing cyber criminals at a national and international level, working proactively to target criminal vulnerabilities and prevent criminal opportunities, assisting the NCA and wider law enforcement to pursue those who utilize the Internet or ICT for criminal means. This includes offering technical, strategic and intelligence support to local and regional law enforcement, as well as supporting the training of the Cyber-crime Units within each ROCU. The Unit driving a step-change in the UK's overall capability to tackle cyber-crime, supporting partners in industry and law enforcement to better protect themselves against cyber-crime.[41]

There are several ways to view the evolution of UK society. Some sociologists view things through scientific glasses while others take an intellectual approach in perceiving the dynamics of social transformation. When it comes to security and terrorism, there are thousands of research papers, essays, speeches and lectures available on the websites of think tanks, newspapers, journals and libraries that address the crisis of national security with different approaches, but there is no coordination. However, some aspects of controversial intelligence and surveillance mechanism also need to be elucidated. As we have already attested, the arrival of new surveillance technologies and their controversial use have badly failed to intercept jihadists joining the ranks of the Islamic State of Iraq and Syria (ISIS) and other groups in the Middle East and South Asia and have been unable to block them coming back.[42]

We also understand that with the introduction of modern communication systems, surveillance and espionage networks have become a global phenomenon. The capturing, tracing and processing of the personal data of citizens have become a controversial issue worldwide. Every state has promulgated its own communication and surveillance law that allows interception of communication and stops e-mail trafficking and monitors Face book, Twitter and YouTube conversations. While we discuss these law enforcement related issues, many new things come to mind: mass surveillance is not a good

---

[41] On November 6, 2014, *The Guardian* reported that Sir Bernard Hogan-Howe, commissioner of the Metropolitan police in London, told a conference of senior US police chiefs that law enforcement agencies in the UK had lost the public's trust after the disclosures on government surveillance made by Mr. Edward Snowden

[42] *Daily Times*, 18 November 2014

solution to our social problems. The focus of intelligence agencies on international terrorism, and specific communities within the country has been a matter of great concern as this way of ethnicized and sectarianized intelligence operation continues to alienate the citizens from the state.

Yes, we know that modern state machinery in the UK ultimately depends on surveillance data but the way surveillance is used against the privacy of citizens has prompted deep frustration and social alienation. The UK's citizens are well aware of their privacy rights protected by international law, but the law in the country has a weak and fractured approach towards privacy. Communities complain that the current legal and regulatory system is not providing adequate protection for personal information. At present, in the UK, the multi-faceted surveillance strategy has become flawed and needs to be reformed to ensure that the right of privacy in the European Convention on Human Rights is honored.

Article eight of the European Convention on Human Rights provides everyone with the right to respect for his private and family life, his home and his correspondence, and that there shall be no interference by a public authority with the exercise of this right except such as is in accordance with the law. In our society, due to the evolving nature of the Interception Communication Law and Regulation of Investigatory Power Act 2000 (ICLRIPA), privacy has become a joke while the Data Protection Act and RIPA have never explained to the citizens what happens to their personal information.

This approach is very weak and the trust between the state's security apparatus, law enforcement agencies and the citizens has been undermined. On 06 November, 2014, The Guardian reported Sir Bernard Hogan-Howe, commissioner of the Metropolitan police in London, told a conference of senior police chiefs that law enforcement agencies in the UK lost the public's trust after the disclosures on government surveillance made by Mr. Edward Snowden. "We need to ensure that where law enforcement accesses private communications there is a process of authorization, oversight and governance that gets the balance right between the individual's right to privacy and their right to be protected from serious crime," said the police chief. But the issue is quite different as the police are not fully cooperating with communities.[43]

The government and its agencies are deeply frustrated due to the looming security crisis and widening sphere of extremism and foreign espionage around us. The intelligence war is another quagmire the country has been entrapped in. British agencies are fighting in different directions against this abruptly imposed war. We know the UK intelligence gained professional experience in countering terrorism and foreign espionage during the last 100 years, but this time, they face the most professionally trained and technologically adorned terrorist networks. The increasing number of dangers transcending national boundaries is a reflection of the government's weak approach to law enforcement and counter-terrorism. An evolving Asian, African and European intelligence policy towards the UK raises several questions, including the recent attitude of France, China, Russia and Germany. Germany cancelled a Cold War era pact with the UK in response to the revelations of Mr. Edwards Snowden about electronic surveillance operations.

In September 2014, former Prime Minister David Cameron said his government was considering introducing some national security measures. These included confiscating the passports of UK extremists, excluding them from the country and placing them on no-fly list arrangements on a statutory footing, but the Prime Minister was unable to fully implement these security measures. Social scientists and independent experts confirmed that the UK's counter-terrorism strategy was failing to tackle the danger of violent extremism and international terrorism. These experts attributed this failure to the controversial approach of counter-terrorism and domestic extremism strategy. As the national security environment for the UK has changed, the country perceives its national security threat emanates from the terrorist and jihadist groups of the Middle East and South Asia.[44]

To tackle all the above-mentioned threats, government and its agencies needed to adopt policies based on the principles of UK culture. We need laws based on our culture and social principles. We do not need to follow the US or European way of countering terrorism. We need to stick to our cultural and social way of

---

[43] On November 26, 2014, the UK's counter-terrorism police warned that the country would be at a heightened risk of terrorism for many years to come.
[44] *Daily Mail* 25 November 2014, and details of National Crime Agency website

countering radicalization; we don't need to follow the US designed counter-terrorism strategies. Notwithstanding Whitehall's very robust commitment towards protecting the UK citizens from any abrupt terrorist attack, public confidence, trust and satisfaction between the police and communities have steadily declined. The Prime Minister allocated about 130 million pounds for MI5 to help identify lone wolves, and vowed to give more power to MI5 and MI6 for tackling domestic and international terrorism. In the new counter-terrorism and security bill, some measures were also added including the countering of radicalization and powers to stop people heading abroad to join the Islamic State (IS) networks in Syria and Iraq.

The coverage regarding the failure of British way of policing printed in newspapers and electronic media is typically perceived as more credible than the braying of our politicians and Ministers. The list of threats and security gaps are endless, ranging from lone wolves returning from the Middle East and South Asia to the trends of jihadism across the country. Sectarianism fuels the most violent threat to peace and security. Pakistani sectarian mullahs are making things worse by igniting sectarianism in their Friday prayer. Recently, parliament's intelligence and security committee inquiry into how terrorists killed a UK soldier in East London, termed it as an intelligence failure. The inquiry also warned that the existing government strategies that aim to undermine extremism were not working as 1,000 radicalized Muslims reached Iraq and Syria for jihad.

As extremist and jihadist forces encircled us from all sides, we remain in the middle; neither can we go back nor can we proceed to our destination. On November 26, 2014, the UK's counter-terrorism police warned that the country could be at a heightened risk of terrorism for many years to come. Mr. Mark Rowley revealed that his department experienced many terror-related incidents during 2014: "We are facing a threat that is very different to what we have faced before in terms of its scale and nature, and at the moment the Internet is a big part of that."[45]

Deputy leader of the UK's Labor Party, Mr. Khaled Mahmood, also expressed deep concern over the involvement of 2,000 UK jihadists in the sectarian conflict of the Middle East. Mr. Khaled criticized the government for its controversial border control mechanism. The borders of the country are not obstacles for jihadists returning home.

[45] Ibid.

A former police officer warned that people who sneaked under the police radar for jihad abroad were coming back through inadequate immigration controls at UK airports. The UK and the European Union states have been increasingly anxious about their countries turning into domestic extremism and ISIS-recruiting hubs. "The increasing threat we face including from these so-called self-starting terrorists means that we should now go further in strengthening our capabilities," former Prime Minister David Cameron told parliament.[46]

The government and law enforcement agencies were on the run; the Prime Minister herself was discontented over the intensified process of radicalization, while the Home Secretary was confused about how to tackle this hydra. The UK's mujahedeen were arriving here one by one, with new ideas, a fresh zeal and a brand new mentality from the training camps of the ISIS. They represented ISIS here and acted on the behalf of Abu Bakr al-Baghdadi, leader of the organization. This is what Mark Rowley described as a different kind of threat in scale and nature. In view of these developments, the government announced new counter-terrorism measures, including a range of powers to block suspected UK jihadists from returning home. The Home Office used to seek the cooperation of intelligence agencies to intercept possible terror attacks. Home Secretary warned, "We are in the middle of a generational struggle against a deadly terrorist ideology."[47]

She repeatedly described these concerns in her speech at the Royal United Services Institute for Strategic Studies: "Since the start of this government, the counter-terrorism Internet referral unit has secured the removal of 65,000 items from the Internet that encouraged or glorified acts of terrorism. More than 46,000 of these have been removed since December last year. At present, content relating to IS, Syria and Iraq represents around 70 percent of the unit's caseload. "Since I became home secretary, I have excluded hundreds of people, in total, from the UK. I have excluded 61 people on national security grounds and 72 people because their presence here would not have been conducive to the public good. In total, I have excluded 84 hate preachers. Seventy-four organizations are at present proscribed because they are engaged in, or support, terrorism."[48]

---

[46] *Daily Times*, 02 December 2014
[47] *Telegraph*, 22 January 2017
[48] *The Guardian* 24 August 2016

The failure of the Metropolitan police to address the social pain of communities and control crime has resulted in mistrust between the police and communities. It was widely debated in print and electronic media in the country. The civil society was of the view that million CCTV cameras, mass surveillance, and watchdog organizations from skies to the underground failed to deliver positively and show that they were operating in the right direction.

Sectarian conflict in Northern Ireland received little attention worldwide as violence continues to inflict fatalities on residents of the province. There are numerous books, research papers and article available in libraries that spotlight the level of violence and government approach to law and order mechanism. The threat level in the province is revolving based on the operational strategies of both the IRA and government forces. In 2015 and 2016, police in the province recorded 36 shooting incidents, all but half of the number recorded in the previous years. In the same period there were 52 bomb blasts incidents, in which hundreds of civilians were killed. Police recovered more than 66 firearms and 4,418 round of ammunition.[49]

On 22 January 2017, Guardian reported a police officer was shot by terrorists in Northern Ireland.[50] On 24 August 2016, a royal marine was arrested over a terrorist plot.[51] Moreover, Northern Ireland Secretary James Brokenshire said 103 people were arrested in connection with terrorism. Vigilance urged as Northern Ireland terror threat 'remains severe.[52] The issue of the emergence of New IRA occurred to be irksome for the UK police department as the group started military activities in Northern Ireland and Dublin. This is a new violent group fighting for the annexation of Northern Ireland to Republic of Ireland since years. Amidst this prevailing fear, counter terrorism police on 05 August 2016 uncovered a major dissident arms and ammunition dump.[53]

---

[49] Chief Constable's Formal report, Northern Ireland Policing Board 9th June 2016, *Belfast Telegraph*, 06 December 2016

[50] Police Service of Northern Ireland Recorded Security Situation Statistics Annual Report Covering the period 1st April 2015-31st March 2016, Published on 12 May 2016 https://www.psni.police.uk/globalassets/inside-the-psni/our-statistics/security-situation-statistics/2016/may/annual-security-situation-statistics-report-2015-16.pdf

[51] *The Guardian*, 22 January 2017

[52] *BBC*, 25 August 2016

[53] *International Business Times*, 05 August 2016

A Home Office spokesperson once said that the current terror threat level was severe, which meant that the attacks were highly likely because the exponentially growing terror networks, extremism, jihadism and foreign espionage were spreading across the country, complicating the task of the policing authorities. The irony being that the criminal justice system also faced a set of challenges. Therefore, the crime rate was rising by the day. The police department mostly depended upon drone surveillance and other electronic means in response to the prevailing criminal culture in the country, but the results were underwhelming. Cyber terror networks were looting important data from industry, banking sectors, and state institutions, while we never heard in print and electronic media that a foreign cyber terrorist was arrested.

In 2015, we were told that a reform package was being introduced to improve the performance of the force and make it accountable to communities, but it generated many stories. On many occasions, unfortunately, every reformer tried to paint a positive image of the police force in society but failed due to unknown hindrances. In 2012, former Home Secretary (Prime Minister) Theresa May told us that she had commissioned Tom Winsor to carry out a full independent review of police miseries as the existing pay system was designed 30 years ago, in which police officers were unable to pay either their mortgages or spend on family members wholeheartedly.[54]

In 2012, a chapter of police and crime commissioner was also introduced by the government to make efficient the force. Now the commissioner became an elected officer. In November 2012, the first commissioner was elected and after four years, in May 2016, another was elected. Before all these decisions, Home Office published a consultation paper on the government vision of policing, and the police and crime commissioners. However, the police reforms and social responsibility bill was also introduced to identify the core function of the police forces in the UK.[55]

After a deep study of the police department, Winsor presented a comprehensive outline, but a response to his first report was

---

[54] Police Pay: Winsor Review Updated in 2015. Tom Winsor conducted an independent review of police officers and staff remuneration and condition, Part-1 Report, March 2011. https://www.gov.uk/government/uploads/system/uploads/attachment_data/file/229006/8024.pdf

[55] *Telegraph*, 16 November 2012

not satisfactory as the police arbitration tribunal explicitly made no decision. She said that the Home Office was leaving no stone unturned to change the fate of the police, but policing experts noted that organized crime cost Britain 40 billion a year, in which more than 40,000 criminals of 7,000 gangs were involved.[56] Drug trafficking, human trafficking, foreign espionage, terror-related networks, modern slavery, sexual exploitation, irregular migration, corruption, racism, discrimination, poverty, illiteracy, and international terrorism made the lives of British citizens underwhelming and melancholy. In all these cases, the police response was very poor. On 19 January 2017, Metropolitan Police Commissioner, Sir Bernard Hogan-Howe warned that the latest rise in violent crime across England and Wales was a matter of great concern. Target killing and murder rose to 22 percent. However, children as young as 12, the police said, were running drugs trade from London to their own countries.[57]

Councilors from 19 boroughs had called on the Home Secretary to undermine this business, in which big gangs exploit children. In a letter to Home Office, they warned that the crisis is going to worsen. Recent crime figure showed 12 million crimes committed in England and Wales in 2016.[58] The letter stated, "We believe that county Lines has the potential to be the next grooming scandal, following the child sexual exploitation scandals we have seen in Rotherham, Oxfordshire and elsewhere in recent years".[59] In 2016, we also experienced the largest conglomeration of extremists in Europe, where they carried out attacks against civilian and government installations that killed hundreds of innocent citizens. These elements belonging to more than 100 countries gathered in major cities and were adorned with bombs and guns. The interesting news in 2016 was that the UK intelligence and counter-terrorism authorities foiled more than 10 fatalistic terrorist attacks. It means terrorists have encircled us from all sides.

The future of the UK police operations has, once more, moved to the centre of the political battleground. The Cameron government weakened it by interfering in its infrastructure, but, to some

---

[56] *Daily Times*, 24 January 2017
[57] Ibid.
[58] *Sputnik News* 19 January 2017
[59] Ibid.

extent, introduced some reforms. The police need further reforms as the force has been divided on ethnic bases, which cannot operate wholeheartedly. This divide and the attitude of some stakeholders made the police reluctant to face the exponentially growing nature of terror-related crimes. Deteriorating relationship between police forces, and politicians, increasingly characterized by mutual suspicion. Politicians want more space in the policing infrastructure.

During the last 150 years of the establishment of the UK police force (1829) and the establishment of the police complaints board in 1977, no independent oversight was existed in dealing with complaints in the country. Although royal commission on the police that reported in 1962 come about as a result of the widely publicized dismissal of several officers in corruption and fraud cases: "The police a disciplined body, and proper leadership requires that the administration of justice should be in the hands of the chief constable. Any whittling down of this responsibility would weaken the chief constable's command of the force and this again would lead to a loss of moral and confidence".[60]

There are so many key weaknesses in the police reform act notwithstanding the improvement that the government made, the system dealing with complaints is deeply complicated, bureaucratic and slow. This system does not meet the expectation of communities. There are so many challenges faced by complainants against the police misconduct, notwithstanding the principles of the Taylor reforms in 2008, which empowers local management to deal with the issue. The UK police face numerous challenges due to the recent budget cuts, which include reviewing the role of neighborhood policing. The exponentially growing graph of extremism and radicalization has put the police forces on the ordeal. In a modern state, policing is a diverse job, which requires a disciplined approach and public confidence. Many police forces adopt different approaches like conduct policy, and disciplinary procedure.

We live in an age of risk mixed insecurities, anxieties about civilities and anti-social behavior. We hope, policing and intelligence forces will respond to all these torments and threats with a professional security approach in maintaining security and law and order. The

---

[60] Towards greater public confidence: A proposal review of the current police complaints system for England and Wales, Deborah Glass, March 2016

chapter on social media added to the law enforcement operation in the UK, though strengthen the resolve of the police, but it also needs a new approach to counter the criminal culture that has emerged from Face book, YouTube, Twitter and other online sources. Intelligence-led policing can be more effective.[61]

---

[61] *Daily Times*, 07 February 2017

Chapter 3. Policing, Islamic State, Radicalization and Counter-Terrorism

The technological revolution in the field of information collection and analysis has brought about important changes, making states vulnerable to new risks. In Britain and Europe, state and private computers can be targeted from safe distances, within the region or from outside. These technologies have significant implications for law enforcement in general, and in the area of crime prevention and crime detection in particular.

In order to understand the sensitivities of information technologies and their use, we need to understand the use of security computers. Recent terrorist attacks in EU and the Middle East show that terrorists can use modern technologies in their operations.

The London and Manchester attacks showed that terrorists have recruited young jihadists, sent them to Syrian and Iraq for jihad, and used them inside the UK for terrorist attacks. These attacks proved that the UK's preventive strategy has failed to address the threat of jihadism and extremism. Radicalized elements are walking around unfazed, and openly threaten those criticizing their illegal activities. Pakistani journalist Zahid Hussain (2017) views radicalization in the UK as a very real threat:

> Days after the deadly explosion at an arena in Manchester, where American pop singer Ariana Grande had been performing, three attackers rammed their van into a weekend crowd at London Bridge and then knifed multiple people. The two incidents left dozens of people dead and wounded. The perpetrators were all home-grown

radicals with their families originating from different Muslim states. This also raises the question about the trajectory of radicalization of those murderers. None of them seems to have been trained in terrorist camps abroad. Not surprisingly, all three attacks were claimed by the IS, though there is no clarity over how they were linked to the terrorist group. Indeed, they reflected a copycat trend influenced by strong IS propaganda. The latest surge in terror strikes has come when the ISIS is being driven out of territories under its control in Iraq and Syria. But this was not the first time that the terrorists used a speeding van to kill pedestrians. The London Bridge attack echoed earlier carnages perpetrated by speeding vehicles last year in Nice where crowds were celebrating Bastille Day and at a Christmas market in Berlin.[62]

Pakistanis living in Britain have established numerous extremist networks. They recruit people to fight in Kashmir and Afghanistan. They have also established a chain of mosques and religious schools, and collect funds for their mujahedeen. Mr. Zahid Hussain highlighted the life, origin and activities of a Pakistani extremist who killed innocent civilians in London:

> Salman Abedi, the 22-year-old man whose family hails from Libya, came into contact with the group during a visit to his homeland. Khurram Butt was reported for his radical Islamic views. A football fan with two small children, Butt's journey to becoming a mass murderer remains a subject of investigation. Son of parents from Jhelum, Butt was born in Pakistan but brought up in Britain. He was described by his neighbors in east London as a keen supporter of the Arsenal football club whose shirt he wore during the attack. Last month, he was spotted urging people not to participate in the general elections. But no one suspected him of planning to commit mass murder. The other attacker, a Moroccan, did not seem to have any history of association with radical activity. The poster on the IS website may have motivated an already radicalized mind to act.[63]

Analyst Noman Sattar also noted the trends of radicalization and extremism in Europe and the United Kingdom, and briefly discussed the London and Manchester terrorist acts:

> The current wave of terrorism has focused on western Europe. The last few years have seen deadly attacks in France, Belgium, Germany — the heart of western Europe, and England; England has seen a prolonged wave of terrorism in the last century. In the current

---

[62] *Dawn*, 07 June 2017
[63] Ibid.

wave, one could start with the July 7, 2005 London Underground attacks, killing 38. These attacks shook the island nation. This was the beginning. With a huge Muslim immigrant population, ripe to be radicalized for different reasons, one could assume local recruitment and sleeper cell activity. Then came March 2017, and the Westminster Bridge attacks broke the lull. The incident was rather bizarre, carried out by an individual with the location also reflecting a new strategy... This attack brought terrorism to the forefront of national discourse in England. And there was more to come. On May 23 in Manchester a suicide bombing at a concert claimed the lives of 22 people. This attack followed the pattern of the terrorist attacks in France. Isis claimed responsibility but this attack too was apparently carried out by an individual from an immigrant Libyan family.[64]

After the Manchester attacks, Prime Minister Theresa May insisted that world leaders needed to do more to combat online extremism. The UK Government defined extremism as vocal or active opposition to fundamental British values, including democracy, the rule of law, individual liberty and mutual respect and tolerance of different faiths and beliefs.

Evidence shows that more unequal societies have lower levels of social cohesion those more equal societies. Those with greater wealth tend to have less empathy for others. Collectively, we have less trust in not only our political institutions, but also other individuals and communities. On 07 June 2017, the Guardian reported Prime Minister Theresa May warned that there had been "far too much tolerance of extremism" in the UK and, promised to step up the fight against Islamist terrorism after the London Bridge attack, saying "enough is enough". Prime Minister May said Internet companies must not allow extremism a place to exist, but added that there was also a need to tackle "safe spaces in the real world", which would require "difficult" conversations.[65]

The Prime Minister also suggested the idea of increased prison terms for terrorism offenses, even relatively minor ones. Islamist militancy was the thread that linked the otherwise unconnected attacks in London Bridge, Westminster and Manchester, she said. The newspaper reported. "As terrorism breeds terrorism and perpetrators are inspired to attack, not only on the basis of carefully constructed plots after years of planning and training, and not even

---

[64] *The News* 07 2017
[65] On 07 June 2017, *the Guardian* reported Prime Minister Theresa May warned that there had been "far too much tolerance of extremism" in the UK

as lone attackers radicalized online, but by copying one another and often using the crudest of means of attack," the Prime Minister said.[66]

More than 1,000 radicalized elements from the UK joined the ISIS in Syria and Iraq, and 50% of these fighters returned. In fact, government failed to address the issue of radicalization and extremism. The UK counter terrorism authorities, Home Office and intelligence agencies have been unable to control this hydra as it come out of its nest and target innocent civilians time and again. The range of measures used to challenge extremism in the UK include: preventing "apologists" for terrorism and extremism from travelling to the UK, giving guidance to local authorities and institutions, funding a specialist police unit which works to remove online content that breaches terrorist legislation, the Counter Terrorism Internet Referral Unit.[67]

Government supports community-based campaigns and activity to rebut terrorist and extremist propaganda and offer alternative views to vulnerable target audiences, working with a range of civil society organizations, but these measures are inadequate to address this issue. Baroness Shields, the Minister for Internet Safety and Security, described ISIL and other groups as operating a "dispersed network of accounts". Homegrown terrorism inspired by the Islamic State poses threat to the United Kingdom's national security.[68]

Expert Mr. Soeren Kern discusses the report on the Gatestone Institute website: "The 1,000-page report 'Islamist Terrorism: Analysis of Offenses and Attacks in the UK (1998–2015)' was published on March 5 by the Henry Jackson Society, a foreign policy think tank based in London. The report, authored by terrorism researcher Hanna Stuart, identifies profiles and analyzes all 269 Islamism-inspired terrorism convictions and suicide attacks in the United Kingdom between 1998 and 2015. The report also compares data between 1998 and 2010, a period when al-Qaeda reached its zenith, and 2011 and 2015, the period following the death of Osama bin Laden in May 2011, the uprisings known as the Arab Spring, and the rise of the Islamic State in 2014".[69]

---

[66] Ibid.

[67] Radicalization: the counter-narrative and identifying the tipping point. British Parliament August 2016. https://www.publications.parliament.uk/pa/cm201617/cmselect/cmhaff/135/13504.htm

[68] Ibid.

[69] Gatestone Institute, 07 March 2017,Mr. Soeren Kern analysis

The UK police department maintains law and order uninterruptedly by using CCTV cameras, Face book, YouTube, Flicker, Pinterest, Google, Audiobook and Twitter, which failed to address the exponentially growing radicalization and extremism. This electronic approach to law enforcement has always ignored the importance of human intelligence that plays significant role in security and stability of a state. These tools allow Britain's police to engage in law enforcement with transformative ways. Since the creation of World Wide Web in 1991, Internet became an important tool for promoting radicalization and extremism. Terrorist organization use Internet to streamline their activities and carry out coordinated attacks against the government and civilian targets.[70]

National Security Strategy of the United Kingdom was published in 2010, which identified terrorism in a specific way. The terrorism act 2000 provides the legal basis for prosecuting terrorists and proscribing organizations. The Protection of Freedoms Act 2012 repealed the stop and search powers known as 'Section 44' and replaced them with fairer and more specific powers. The new stop and search powers enable the police to protect the public but also make sure that there are strong safeguards to prevent a return to the previous excessive use of stop and search without suspicion.

The Protection of Freedoms Act 2012 also reduced the maximum period that a terrorist suspect could be detained before they are charged or released from 28 to 14 days. Control orders were repealed and replaced with a more streamlined and less intrusive system. In December 2011 the Terrorism Prevention and Investigations Measures Act introduced the new system of terrorism prevention and investigation measures. The government also published a draft Communications Data Bill on 14 June 2012. A Joint Committee of both Houses of Parliament scrutinized the draft Bill and reported on 11 December 2012. The Intelligence and Security Committee also conducted its own inquiry into the draft Bill and published its full report.

In their findings, both committees recognized the need for new laws. The Data Retention and Investigatory Powers Act (DRIPA) were passed in July 2014. The legislation was brought forward after

[70] United Nations Counter-Terrorism Implementation Task Force Working Group Compendium Countering, the Use of the Internet for Terrorist Purposes —Legal and Technical Aspects, May 2011, United Nations Department of Political Affairs Counter-Terrorism Implementation Task

the European Court of Justice declared the European Data Retention Directive (which formed the basis of the 2009 UK regulations governing the retention of communications data by communication service providers) invalid. The Act maintains the status quo by providing a clear basis in UK law for the retention of communications data; however its provisions expire at the end of 2016.[71]

Former Prime Minister David Cameron authorized an investigation into the illegal funds of UK-based extremist jihadist groups, while Foreign Secretary Philip Hammond dramatically revealed that more than 600 radicalized Britons had been intercepted going for jihad to Syria. "Approximately 800 have made it through since 2012, with half of them still thought to be inside the war torn country," Philip Hammond said.[72] Metropolitan Police faces unprecedented difficulty in dealing with these jihadists and racism across the country. In 2011, the failure of Metropolitan Police to manage and control criminal gangs and their violent actions on the streets of London raised serious questions about the competency and credibility of the force. To improve the operational capability and remove the prevailing misunderstanding regarding the police force, Mr. Tom Winsor was assigned the task of conducting an independent review of police officers and staff remuneration and conditions, which was published on 08 March 2011.[73]

The British National Counter Terrorism and Security Office (NPCC) has developed expertise to tackle radicalization and terrorism, and brings police forces in the UK together to help policing coordinate operations, and reform. The biggest threats to public safety are national and international. The NPCC has a collective strength by coordinating the operational response across forces. Its main function is to co-ordinate national operations including defining, monitoring and testing force contributions to the Strategic Policing Requirement working with the National Crime Agency where appropriate, delivery

---

[71] The UK Investigatory Powers Act 2016 – what it will mean for your business, Graham Smith, 29 November 2016

[72] *Daily Times*, 19 January 2016, House of Lords House of Commons Joint Committee on the Draft Investigatory Powers Bill Draft Investigatory Powers Bill, together with formal minutes relating to the report. Published on 11 February 2016 by authority of the House of Lords and House of Commons. https://www.publications.parliament.uk/pa/jt201516/jtselect/jtinvpowers/93/93.pdf,

[73] Securing Cyberspace: International and Asian Perspectives, Editors: Editors Cherian Samuel and Munish Sharma, Institute for Defense studies and Analysis India, 2016

of counter terrorist policing through the national network as set out in the Counter Terrorism Collaboration Agreement, co-ordination of the national police response to national emergencies and the co-ordination of the mobilization of resources across force borders and internationally, the national operational implementation of standards and policy as set by the College of Policing and Government, to work with the College of Policing, to develop joint national approaches on criminal justice, value for money, service transformation, information management, performance management and technology.[74]

The second body of the NPCC is National Police Coordination Centre (NPoCC), which is responsible for coordinating the deployment of police officers and staff from across UK policing to support forces during large scale events, operations and in times of national crisis for example large scale flooding and civil emergencies.[75] The performance of NPCC has been excellent during the last decade, but on 05 June 2017, Prime Minister Theresa May took the unprecedented step of attacking her own track record. She told the press, "The UK has not done enough to defeat extremism, and I should know because it was very specifically my job.[76]

> When I say we haven't done enough, I can be sure I'm correct in that assessment because everything we did for the last six years in trying to tackle extremism went across my desk as Home Secretary, and was specifically approved by me. So when I say we haven't done enough, I am basically saying I was a bit shit at my job for quite a number of years. That's how confident I am about this election; I can openly admit I did a bad job, but you lot will still vote for me because Jeremy Corbyn looks a bit awkward in a suit. "Wonderful, isn't it?" the Prime Minister said.[77]

Now as the Prime Minister admitted her failure, we can safely declare that in the last fifteen years the United Kingdom has failed to tackle jihadism and extremism. The UK has several pieces of terrorism legislation such as the Terrorism Act 2000, the Anti-Terrorism Crime and Security Act 2001, the Prevention of Terrorism Act 2005, the Terrorism Act 2006, the Counter-Terrorism Act 2008

[74] The NPCC brings police forces in the UK together to help policing coordinate operations, reform, improve and provide value for money. http://www.npcc.police.uk/About/AboutNPCC.aspx
[75] Ibid.
[76] On 05 June 2017, Prime Minister Theresa May took the unprecedented step of attacking her own track record in tackling extremism, The Guardian
[77] Ibid.

and the Counter-Terrorism and Security Act 2015, but in spite of all this verbiage, in real life terrorists continue to carry out successful attacks.[78]

By virtue of their executive nature, these and other terrorism powers take place virtually outside the criminal justice system, severely testing the limits of the rule of law. Political Scientist, Dr. Maria Norris criticized the present way of countering terrorism in the UK: "Sixteen years since the first general terrorism act, 15 years since 9/11, 11 years since 7/7, this is what it is like to live in a State that Counters Terror: a society where the state does not trust its citizens and its citizens don't trust the state, or each other. With more terrorism legislation on the way and plans to revoke the Human Rights Act, what kind of society will we become in the next 15 years? That is the question that should be at the forefront of all our minds".[79]

Home Secretary once admitted that Home Office had implemented the majority of Mr. Tom Winsor's recommendations, and further added that there were holes that needed to be tackled, but the case is different. Mr. Tom's recommendations were not implemented while Theresa May left the UK police in hot water. After a thorough investigation into the police reforms, Mr. Tom designed a revised pay structure which could not succeed. Police officers are still unable to manage their family budgets on the miserable pay they receive. The two years freeze on pay increments and hour allowance cannot have helped to change to the minds of many officers. Mr. Tom Winsor's proposal to encourage young people to join the police force also proved ineffective.

Police officers continue to resign due to their working environment and kitchen problems. There is fear that foreign intelligence agents or criminal gangs may possibly infiltrate the police department by applying for jobs. In his 1,000-page report, Mr. Tom maintained that the roots of policing lie in a working class structure. This perception enraged thousands of police officers. Against these reforms, on July 24, 2012, the Police Negotiation Board did not agree to some proposals relating to pay and conditions thus, Mr. Tom Winsor's policing

---

[78] Dr Maria Norris, *The New Statement*, 11 September 2016

[79] Fifteen years on from 9/11, how the UK bypassed justice to become a counter-terrorism state, Dr Maria Norris, *The New Statement*, 11 September 2016, http://www.newstatesman.com/politics/uk/2016/09/fifteen-years-911-how-uk-bypassed-justice-become-counter-terrorism-state

reforms faced strong opposition from some institutions and specific circles.[80]

In 2010, the coalition government in Britain announced a 20 percent reduction in the police budget over a period of four years, which prompted frustration within the force as many police forces began to consider outsourcing key service areas to the private sector to save money. In July 2012, the failure of the G4S in maintaining the Olympics' security generated negative debate in print and electronic media. The debate noted the inability of private security agencies to help the police in maintaining law and order in the country. After reading these disappointing sagas of failed law enforcement strategies, one can understand the fear and irritation of British law enforcement agencies from the fact that due to their shrunk financial recourses, terrorists and foreign espionage networks across the country are making trouble.

In 2014, 3,000 allegations against the UK police were leveled but only 1,500 were investigated. The performance of the government's prevention strategy has been very poor during the last two years. Law enforcement agencies are still unable to infiltrate into the networks of foreign terrorist groups operating in the country. Some research reports recently highlighted a countrywide operation of foreign sponsored human trafficking networks in conjunction with spy networks challenging the authority of law enforcement agencies.[81]

Mr. Edward Snowden also exposed the inability of British policing agencies to intercept radicals joining Islamic State (ISIS). Hate crime, extremism, gangs' networks and the presence of foreign intelligence networks across the country threatened the lives of British citizens. Every day, we experience new incidents of violence and terrorism but British law enforcement agencies (though well-equipped) are unable to respond professionally. To manage law and order, and effectively counter domestic and international terror networks, government needs wide-ranging security sector reforms, and need to learn and manage forces with a professional streak.

The performance of police officers needs deep improvement and the police department needs a professional and educated police force to address the complaints of communities. In view of violent threat from ISIS and extremist groups in the country, Scotland Yard

[80] *The Guardian*, 15 January 2015, Telegraph, 15 January 2016
[81] *Daily Times*, 19 January 2016

doubled the number of armed police patrol. The Met police also boasted a 400-strong specialist squad of firearm officers in 2015. The Scotland Yard chief, Sir Bernard Hogan-Howe announced that he was increasing the total number of trained marksmen by six hundreds.

The role of CCTV cameras in law enforcement is of great importance. These tools are making effective the policing way of operation in the streets and town of the United Kingdom. In fact, CCTV cameras identify crime scene and the action of criminals in streets and market to help the police in arresting anti social elements. However, CCTV cameras were installed in Britain to interdict burglary, robbery, assault, theft, fraud and other traditional crimes, but the use of these cameras become controversial when some communities complained that police uses CCTV against their privacy and social activities. Home Office promotional booklet states that CCTV can be a solution to racial harassment, drug use, sexual harassment and discrimination, but response of the public to this effort has not been positive since the installation of these surveillance cameras.[82]

Fundamentally, one cannot deny the benefits of CCTV cameras, but communities are not satisfied with performance of these systems. Terror-related incidents, robbery, theft, sexual assaults, and attacks on minorities in buses and trains have increased, despite the CCTV cameras that are supposed to help the police in identifying suspects. As I mentioned earlier that CCTV cameras have both positive and negative aspects: in addition to deterring crime, they actually create new crimes in terms of the violation of privacy, in houses, markets and other areas. If we read the details of Cyber Security Strategy of the United Kingdom, we can find both positive and critical information about the function of CCTV cameras. The Cyber Security Strategy acknowledges: "It is not possible to eliminate cyber-crime".[83]

In another report, the BBC (2010) noted people's reservations on the function of CCTV cameras. There are many complaints registered with the prevention of crime council that these cameras just generate fear among local communities and business firms. Muslim Communities

---

[82] In 2014, 3,000 allegations against the UK police were leveled but only 1,500 were investigated. 19 Jan 2016, *Daily Times*
[83] The Crisis of Britain's Surveillance State: Security, Law Enforcement and the Intelligence War in Cyberspace, Musa Khan Jalalzai, Algora Publishing, Riverside, New York, USA, 2014. Also, Issues of Monitoring Cyber Crime-A Growing Challenge for Governments, John Herhalt, *KPMG International*, Volume, 08, July 2011

in the UK often complained against the installation of CCTV cameras in their areas by the police to monitor their religious ceremonies and private lives. They say this also generates misunderstanding between the government and communities. As per my personal observation, these security cameras are, in fact, an invasion on our privacy and private lives. The installations of these cameras in bathrooms and dressing rooms have no justification at all. Yes, the presence of CCTV is of much importance, and it plays significant role protecting public in streets and markets, but the unprofessional use of these tools has prompted some misunderstanding between the law enforcement agencies and communities.[84]

If we look at the positive function of CCTV, we can find that CCTV reduce fear, help the police in investigation, provide technical assistance and gather information. Conversely, literature on the function of CCTV cameras also noted their negative aspects involving displacement, increasing fear and the increase of crime reporting, which is an irksome issue for the police. In communities and markets, their response has been negative since long as they understand these cameras are spying on them. According to a second opinion, the CCTV may possibly increase in recording crime, which is not acceptable for the law enforcement agencies.9 The CCTV cameras also causes of unintended effects, good and bad or false sense of security. Recent research reports have documented the negative aspects of CCTV cameras and their inconclusive prevention capabilities. There are mixed opinions which demand change in the function of the CCTV and changes in surveillance law to make effective the function of these tools.[85]

Some suggest that the main issue is heavy cost on this business, needs to be reduced. Experts understand that the installation of these cameras across the country undermined the traditional concept of policing communities and community policing. They say that in majority crime reports made by CCTV, the police fail to analyze these reports in its true sense. They complain that the CCTV cameras do not work properly, and criminals have baseball caps and hooded tops to hide their faces, and operate quickly. Security Cameras making

[84] CCTV Surveillance, Video Practices and Technology, H Kruegle, Butterworth Heinemanne Books, 15 December 2006
[85] The UK Cyber Security Strategy, November 2011

55

people feel safe falsely, and the robbers robe their house with a modern technique.[86]

The increasing use of CCTV cameras in public domain risk changing the mind of communities about the government attitude towards minorities across the UK. They perceive these cameras in their areas as an act of discrimination and violation of their privacy. The UK Surveillance Commissioner, and a former senior counter-terrorism officer, Toney Porter warned in one of his interview that the police monitoring of people must be in a transparent manner.[87]

On 22 October 2015, in his speech to the Association of Police and Crime Commissioners in London, Surveillance Camera Commissioner, Tony Porter said: "So, there is a disconnect here-in some areas CCTV is valued as an excellent tool for policing elsewhere it's dismissed. I often hear from local authorities CCTV mangers that they never get any feedback from forces on how effective CCTV has been in aiding investigations, arrests, and convictions. How can they evidence its value to their counselors with ever diminishing budget if they are getting no feedback on its effectiveness? How do they know their cameras aren't fit for purpose if no one tells them"?[88]

The majority of the CCTV cameras have failed to deliver properly as we have experience in the past when criminal robbed many houses in East and West London by applying new criminal techniques. The irony is that majority of business and other firms and systems little invested in the duplicate signed copies, sealed evidence bags and others to provide the court with an unbroken chain of evidence. Second, the times and date stamp on the CCTV monitor printout can be fabricated in personal computers because video editing tools are easily available in the market.[89]

Now amid these controversies and complaints, the Information Commissioner's Office (ICO) issued code practice of surveillance under the Data Protection Act 1998, which covers the use of CCTV.

---

[86] The UK Cyber Security Strategy, 2011, and also Cyber Crime and Cyber Security: Key Issues for the 2015 Parliament

[87] The CCTV site Internet Eyes hope to catch criminals, Dhruti Shah, *BBC News*, 2010, also see, the College of Policing, http://library.college.police.uk/docs/what-works/What-works-briefing-effects-of-CCTV-2013.pdf.

[88] Security, Law Enforcement and the Intelligence War in Cyberspace, Musa Khan Jalalzai, Algora Publishing, Riverside, New York, USA, 2014

[89] The effect of CCTV on Public Safety: Research Roundup, Journalist's Resource, 11 February 2014, and also *Journal of Quantitative Criminology*, Volume 30, Issue 2, June 2014

The code was updated in 2008 to bring about concordance between the government and communities. It is estimated that there are over 10 million CCTV cameras operating in the UK, including 750,000 in sensitive locations but the graph of crime and crime-related activities is still there.[90]

The emergence of surveillance technology has confined human being to a limited space. As the criminal culture in the United Kingdom prevailed during the last 15 years, the demand for the CCTV cameras increased. Now, in spite of its benefits, discussion about their negative impacts diverted the attention of Crime Commissioner and law enforcement authorities toward its professional use. In the United Kingdom, CCTV help the police in fighting crime, but sometimes, CCTV fail to identify robbers and serious organized criminals.[91]

Moreover, the CCTV cameras are also eroding our standing democratic right of privacy. In Markets, many companies believe the use of CCTV may help in improvement of their employee's behaviors, but it also creates misunderstanding between the companies' owners and employees. People complain that the CCTV cameras are harmful to their life and privacy. They say that as they are being protected by CCTV, they also feel that they are watched everywhere.[92]

The House of Commons Home affairs Committee on Counter-terrorism in its report (2014-2015) on foreign fighter suggested a five point plan to strengthen the measures already in place: "Improve communication between police, schools and parents are in need of vast improvement. The police must engage in a regular and open dialogue with schools and community groups to ensure that information is exchanged and new initiatives can be explored at community level. The increase in police diversity, and Provide advice, provide a counter-narrative, and improve international co-operation".[93]

---

[90] UK Public must Wake Up to Risks of CCTV, says Surveillance Commissioner, Tony Porter, Matthew Weaver, The Guardian, 06 January 2015, Why Surveillance Cameras don't Reduce Crime, 31 March 2005, Clive Robinson

[91] UK Public must Wake Up to Risks of CCTV, says Surveillance Commissioner, Tony Porter, Matthew Weaver, The *Guardian*, 06 January 2015

[92] The maximum Surveillance Society: The Rise of CCTV, Gary Armstrong, Clive Norris, Bloomsbury, September 1999

[93] Speech to the Association of Police and Crime Commissioners, Mr. Porter outlined PCC's statutory responsibilities in relation to Surveillance Cameras Code of Practice. 22 October 2015, https://www.gov.uk/government/speeches/speech-to-the-association-of-police-and-crime-commissioners-agm-2015, and The Information Commissioner Office website details about the surveillance Cameras, 21 May2015.

CHAPTER 4. INTELLIGENCE SURVEILLANCE, TERFOR STRATEGY AND SECRET AGENCIES

The recent surveillance transformation in the UK has reduced privacy and limited the freedom of speech. Electronic intelligence falls within the domain of state that is responsible to protect national security, but illegal attacks on civilian privacy can alienate them from the state. Lawful interception of communication is based on legal frame work. Data retention and, Regulations of Investigatory Power Act-2014, deals with the retention of communication data.[94] In December 2014, Investigatory Power Tribunal (IPT) said that legal framework in Britain governing the bulk of interception of data is not against human rights law, and is compliant with articles 8 and 10 of the EU convention of human rights.

Intelligence and electronic surveillance of e-mail communication, telephone conversation, websites visits, online shopping, and the whereabouts of people who use cell-phone or keep it in pockets received negative response from communities about the illegal spying strategy of British intelligence agencies. These things prompted many negative impressions and complications for privacy and freedom of expression. Government is free to hack, watch and intercept communication of everyone who uses Internet or cell-phone. After we sent an email to an individual or office, it is stored on server, computer and hard drive. Phone call leave record of conversation and

[94] Data Retention and Investigatory Powers Act 2014.Retention of relevant communications data, the Data Retention and Investigatory Powers Act 2014 received Royal Assent on 17 July. The Act, explanatory notes and impact assessments are available on the Parliament.uk website.

communication with telecommunication companies who share it with government agencies, but all these efforts of the UK surveillance agencies failed to take into confidence communities for their irksome spying.

The intelligence and law enforcement communities of the EU member states are greatly diverse as national laws outlined professional measures for them in the field of intelligence information collection, analysis and in the protection of national critical infrastructure. The culture and infrastructure of intelligence in all EU member states, particularly in Germany, Poland, Romania, Italy, France and Brussels are divided into two separate services, mandated with a domestic and foreign scope. Notwithstanding all these competent aspects of the UK and EU agencies, they have failed to intercept terrorists dancing in the streets of their big cities and towns. European Union Agency for Fundamental Rights elucidated the role of intelligence and the rule of law in democratic societies:

> The more intelligence services shift their activities from state to non-state entities and individual or groups of individuals, as in the case with terrorist's organizations, the more important aspect of the rule of law becomes. The enactment of law is indeed a relatively recent process. The turn to law might have been challenged following the attack in 11 September 2001 on the United States. Recent revelations regarding the intelligence services, surveillance capabilities, however, have underscored the need to respect the fundamental principle of the rule of law in democratic societies.[95]

This is one aspect of different perceptions regarding the evolving function of intelligence and law enforcement mechanism within the EU member states. As mentioned earlier, the fundamental function of British intelligence is not so different from that of the EU member states agencies. What is distinctive is the culture of operational mechanism and changing demonstration within the matrix of the country. As we understand British intelligence by its name and nature, it demonstrates in three different ways. The three intelligence agencies (MI6, MI5, and GCHQ) further divided on small units. These agencies are no doubt skilled and professional but their hands

---

[95] Liberty and Security in a Changing World, *Report and Recommendations of The President's Review Group on Intelligence and Communications Technologies*, 12 December 2013, also; Surveillance by intelligence services: fundamental rights safeguards and remedies in the EU Mapping Member States' legal frameworks, European Union Agency for Fundamental Rights.

are tied by ministerial rope, which confined them to a specific area of operation.

The Intelligence and Security committee (ISC) is scrutinizing these agencies and their activities. The Justice and Security Act 2013 reformed the ISC, making it committee of parliament, providing greater power and increasing its remit. Parliament's Intelligence and Security Committee represents MI5, MI6, GCHQ, Defense Intelligence Staffs and Joint Intelligence Committee in the Cabinet Office. In its website, the Intelligence and Security committee outlined its core legal and administrative function:

> Intelligence and Security Committee of Parliament (ISC) was first established by the Intelligence Services Act 1994 to examine the policy, administration and expenditure of the Security Service, Secret Intelligence Service (SIS) and the Government Communication Headquarters (GCHQ). The Justice and Security Act 2013 reformed the ISC, making it Committee of Parliament, providing greater power and increasing its remit (including oversight of operational activities and the wider intelligence and security activities of government). Other than the three intelligence and security agencies, the ISC examines the intelligence related work of the Cabinet Office including: the Joint Intelligence Committee (JIC), the Assessment Staff; and the National Security Secretariat. The Committee also provides oversight of Defense Intelligence in the Ministry of Defense and the Office for Security and Counter Terrorism in the Home Office.[96]

There are numerous intelligence agencies and units in government and private sectors that provide security to the people of Britain. Private intelligence and security agencies help state agencies in intelligence informational collection and surveillance, in investigation and policing, but the issue of oversight in private security and intelligence agencies is difficult to understand with a sweeping generalization as their system of operation is complicated. The UK Joint Intelligence Committee (JIC) is a state institution that assesses events and situation relating to external affairs, defense, terrorism, and major international criminal activities. It also monitors British interests and review security threats. This committee oversees the setting of

---

[96] Section 215 of the Surveillance Act was amended, which demands the business record, while the Foreign Intelligence Surveillance Act (FISA) did not grant the government any authority to compel the production of such records. Executive Order 12333, Sections 215 and 702 of the Surveillance Act, Electronic Privacy Information Centre.

priorities for MI6, MI5 and GCHQ. In the field of Surveillance and legislation, Regulation of Investigatory Power Act 2000 (RIPA) is an important institution which provides framework of technique.

The United Kingdom maintains the strongest surveillance system supporting security agencies and the police in maintaining law and order in the country. The GCHQ's surveillance sword is TEMPORA, the guardian of Britain's frontier, and the competent tool in combating terrorism and radicalization in the country. Information Commissioner is another important institution that helps law enforcement agencies in securing the state. In its recent report (2016) Information Commissioner has outlined its responsibilities:

> The IC is responsible for promoting and enforcing the Data Protection Act 1998 (DPA), the Freedom of Information Act 2000 (FOIA), and associated legislation are including the Privacy and Electronic Communications Regulations 2003 (PECR) and Environmental Information Regulations 2004 (EIR). The IC promotes the protection of personal information by increasing public awareness, by providing good practice guidance to organizations and by taking remedial action when the DPA is breached.[97]

The issue of Interception of Communications Commissioner (IoCC) and its role is widely discussed in intellectual forums in the United Kingdom. The IoCC role and its oversight is seen a controversial and a role that in many cases alienating citizens. The commissioner claims that, under Part 1, Chapter 1 of the Regulation of Investigatory Power Act 2000, its role is to provide statutory independent oversight of the lawful interception of communication, but also asserts that it also investigate complaints. But, civil society does not agree with this opinion while citizens of the UK are in a dire situation where they also face a rash of mass surveillance agencies, which use covert surveillance, intrusive and directed surveillance. The OSC function is not so different from that of Intelligence Surveillance Commissioner (ISC). The OSC use human intelligence sources under the police act 1997 and part-11 and pat-111 of RIPA. All these institutions are helping the state in maintaining security and stability, and provide important

---

[97] The NSA Report: Liberty and Security in a Changing World, The President's Review Group on Intelligence and Communications Technologies, Richard A. Clarke, Michael J. Morell, Geoffrey R. Stone, Cass R. Sunstein, Peter Swire, Princeton University Press, 31 Mar 2014

information to intelligence agencies. The Justice and Security Act 2013 give more functions to the Intelligence Surveillance Commissioner.[98]

The introduction of mass surveillance systems by the UK and EU intelligence agencies generated a countrywide debate on the right of civilians to be protected from illegitimate or warrantless collection and analysis of their data and metadata. Newspapers and human rights forums in Britain published numerous reports, in which experts expressed concerns about the privacy of citizens. However, the increasing concern of citizens about the right of their privacy has also been reported in print and electronic media, but their voice was never heard. Google, YouTube, Twitter and Face-book continue to violate the rights of their users. They are operating like intelligence agencies, collect and note every piece of civilian interaction and conversation.

A coalition of organizations, "Don't Spy on US" in its policy paper (September 2014) highlights the existing attacks of surveillance and intelligence forces on civilian's privacy in the EU and the UK:

In summer 2013 it was revealed that GCHQ was routinely intercepting undersea fiber-optic cables containing private communication of millions of British residents (the 'TEMPORA' program). The reported scale of the interception is staggering: each day, GCHQ accesses some 21 pet-bytes of data-the equivalent of down loading the entire British Library 192 times.[99]

The GCHQ's interception of the fiber-optic cable network is the digital equivalent of opening all the mail going in and out of the UK on a daily basis. It is surveillance on an industrial scale; surveillance to rival that of the Great Wall of China, surveillance that affects the privacy of almost every person in the UK who uses the Internet and that of outsiders who contact anyone in the UK. None of it has ever been authorized by a judge and yet it cannot be challenged in open court. Its existence was not revealed by any of the statutory oversight commissioners or parliament's Intelligence and Security Committee — but by a foreign whistleblower.

TEMPORA is the surveillance tool that the Government Communication Headquarters (GCHQ) used in the past. TEMPORA has the strongest communication and information collection capabilities to extract information from fiber-optic cables. TEMPORA was created to intercept communication and find access to a large

---

[98] *Daily Times*, 03 March 2015
[99] A coalition of organizations, Don't Spy on us, *policy paper*, September 2014

amount of Internet users' personal data without any individual suspicion or targeting.

Edward Snowden noted in his statement in 2016 that TEMPORA maintained two principal components called Mastering the Internet (MTI) and Global Telecoms Exploitation (GTE). These two components collect information from telephonic conversations and deliver to its headquarters.

As we know that GCHQ is the strongest intelligence agency across Europe, we also understand that it produce large amount of Metadata. Some intelligence experts maintain that GCHQ is stronger than the US NSA agency, because its surveillance system TEMPORA has access to all Internet, telephone, Face book and E-mail communications across Europe. TEMPORA comprised different components codenamed POKERFACE and the XKEYSCORE.

In his TV interview in 2016, Snowden revealed that a new surveillance system operated by the US NSA and the UK GCHQ was called MUSCULAR. MUSCULAR is one of at least 4 other programs that relied on a trusted program known as WINDSTOP. There were newspapers reports in 2012 and 2013, that MUSCULAR collected 181 million records, while INCENSER collected 14 million records. The Washington Post report indicated that MUSCULAR program was strong in data collection than PRISM. MUSCULAR is free to collect data as much it want, and does not need warrants. Moreover, MUSCULAR also supporting the NSA's PINWALE surveillance system in data collection.[100]

The US and UK are under severe criticism from domestic and international privacy and human rights groups on their pushy methods of intelligence surveillance and spying on their own citizens. The CIA, National Security Agency (NSA) and Government Communications Headquarters' (GCHQ's) recent way of interception communication have been deeply irksome to families and business communities in the UK. The GCHQ's interception of the fiber-optic cable network,

---

[100] Edward Snowden in his TV interview in 2016 revealed that a new surveillance system operated by the US NSA and the UK GCHQ is called MUSCULAR. MUSCULAR is one of at least 4 other programs that rely on trusted program known as WINDSTOP. There were newspapers reports in 2012 and 2013, MUSCULAR collected 181 million records, while INCENSER collected 14 million records. The Washington Post report indicates that MUSCULAR program is strong in data collection than PRISM. MUSCULAR is free to collect data as much it want, and does not need warrants. Leaked memos reveal GCHQ efforts to keep mass surveillance secret. *The Guardian*, 25 October 2013

which is the digital equivalent of opening all the post going in and out of the UK, has become a central debate in print and electronic media. In the US, the issue of surveillance mechanism is very complicated.

The US and UK agencies are conducting various surveillance programs to effectively counter terrorism in the United States and Europe. On 27 August, 2013, in the United States, in spite of civilian complaints against the violation of their privacy, former President Barak Obama announced the Review Group on Intelligence and Communications Technologies (RGICT), which was welcomed only by his friends while majority members of civil society remained critical. During my study with the University of Stanford (California) and University of Maryland in 2014, I experienced many new things about the operations of intelligence surveillance and geospatial intelligence mechanism in the US.[101] What is happening behind the curtain is quite disturbing.

Immediately after the 9/11 terrorist attacks, President Bush introduced the elaborate and highly detailed — and highly controversial — Patriot Act, which caused many problems in and outside the country. Section 215 of the Surveillance Act was amended, which demands that business records be handed over, while the Foreign Intelligence Surveillance Act (FISA) did not grant government any authority to compel the production of such records. There are innumerable contradictions and flaws in the US intelligence surveillance system, which continue to alienate the citizens from the state. Not everything is going in the right direction with the operational method of Executive Order 12333, Sections 215 and 702 of the Surveillance Act. FISA is not the only legal authority governing foreign intelligence activities; other statutes and executive orders also spread blankets, covering other facets of intelligence operations.[102]

The NSA tracks SIM cards to locate targets for lethal drone strikes, while Taliban and Islamic State (ISIS) commanders protect themselves simply by distributing different SIM cards among their fighters in order to elude their trackers. When they go to meetings, they take out their SIM cards, put them in a bag and mix them up. That effectively blocks real tracking, since, as noted in Executive Order 12333 that instructs intelligence agencies, "Accurate and timely

---

[101] Ibid.
[102] On February 16, 2015, *The Guardian* reported that a man from Liverpool had been charged with attempting to obtain a chemical weapon.

information about the capabilities, intentions and activities of foreign powers, organizations or persons and their agents is essential to informed decision making in the areas of national defense and foreign relations".[103]

After the revelation of NSA whistleblower Edward Snowden, British government intensified the watch-dog and intelligence surveillance system to counter public debates and media criticism. Regulations of Investigatory Power Act 2000 (RIPA), regulates all these things. Moreover, the Data Protection Act of 1998, RIPA, Telecommunication Act 1984, Wireless Telegraphy Act of 2006 and Intelligence Services Act 1994, all have different points of focus but their watch-dog policy is similar. All these laws and agencies are embedded in international policy, such as the European Convention for Human Rights and Fundamental Freedom from 1998.

In the UK, there are dozens of surveillance laws, reverberations and the big drum (TEMPORA), which has many eyes, hears us with dozens of ears, and watches us from a distance. It also has the membership of Five Eyes, an intelligence alliance between Australia, the US, Canada, New Zealand and the UK.

The regulations covering access the GCHQ's access to emails and phone records intercepted by the NSA was termed a breach of human rights law in 2015, by the Investigatory Powers Tribunal (IPT) here in the UK:

> This is a historic victory in the age-old battle for the right to privacy and free expression," said Rachel Logan, Amnesty International UK's legal program director. Until last year, this way of stealing data and information from email was illegal but, this year, UK surveillance agencies started violating surveillance and human rights laws with impunity. This is the critical judgment of the IPT since its inception in 2000. According to the IPT argument, "The regime governing the soliciting, receiving, storing and transmitting by UK authorities of private communications of individuals located in the UK, which have been obtained by US authorities contravened Articles 8 or 10 of the European convention on human rights.[104]

In 2013, newspapers reported the GCHQ routine intercept of submarine fiber-optic cables containing the private communications of millions of UK residents. A recent research report by the Don't Spy on us Campaign noted:

---
[103] *Daily Times*, 12 September 2014
[104] Ibid., *Policy Paper*, 04 December 2013

The Snowden revelations regarding the scope of GCHQ surveillance under TEMPORA have highlighted the use of warrants for the interception of so-called 'external communications' under section 8(4) RIPA (Regulations of Investigatory Power Act, 2000. It is now clear that section 8(4) warrants have been used as the basis for the mass interception by the GCHQ of millions of private communications as well as its bulk collection of communications data.[105] Now the question is; notwithstanding the multifaceted surveillance from the skies and on the earth, and the blanket of TEMPORA, why the threat of terrorism and radicalization intensifies by the day, the answer is that many things are not going in the right direction in the UK.[106]

In the UK, every year, the fluctuation of security threat level become questionable when new jihadist networks are introduced to communities here. These security threat levels remain irksome as we have been unable to tackle the threat of radicalization and extremism. They are sometimes high, sometimes potential and sometimes severe, but no permanent solution has been sought to professionally tackle threatening ideologies. We are living in fear and do not feel secure as these elements are openly dancing in our streets.

They are also involved in serious organized crime to generate funds for the military operations conducted by the Islamic State of Iraq and Syria (ISIS), the Taliban or Lashkar-e-Tayyaba (LeT). Organized crime has deeply affected our financial market while the National Crime Agency (NCA) and police have failed to prevent narco-smugglers and criminal mafia groups from ruining the lives of our communities across the country. The issue is very serious as jihadists are returning from Syria, Iraq, Afghanistan, Pakistan and Bangladesh with a new zeal and radicalized Salafist ideology. There are 1,000 UK citizens fighting for ISIS in Syria and Iraq. The man who beheaded a US journalist, a UK national in Iraq, was one of them. With the arrival of these radicalized young jihadists and perhaps the awakening of jihadists already associated with the sleeper networks of international terrorist and domestic extremist groups, security and law enforcement agencies are facing the real ordeal of maintaining stability in the country. The changing threat level, return of control order and the new amendment to the national security document indicate that the government has failed to tackle the crisis of domestic

---

[105] Amnesty International, 03 July 2015
[106] BBC, 06 February 2015

radicalization. Short term fixes and patch-up jobs are not enough. Real zeal and real solutions are urgently needed.

The National Security Strategy (NSS) has given priority to counter-terrorism and information warfare but there is a gap between the priorities of the government and the private sector. In order to meet the needs of the private sector, government needs to evolve policies to combat the changing security threat. In 2011, government updated the strategy of counter-terrorism that focused on four specific areas. The strategy stressed the need to stop terror attacks and the people who support them. The four key areas are: pursue, prevent, protect and prepare (PPPP). After the killing of a British soldier in East London, priorities changed and a new counter-terrorism strategy was introduced to tackle domestic radicalization. Former Prime Minister David Cameron introduced a new strategy called the Tackling Extremism and Radicalization Task Force (TERFOR) but failed to deliver positively.[107]

The police statistics show that young people continue to make up a disproportionately high number of those arrested for terrorist-related offenses and of those travelling to join terrorist groups in Syria and Iraq. Former Prime Minister David Cameron said: "I said in July that tackling extremism will be the struggle of our generation, one which we will defeat if we work together. All public institutions have a role to play in rooting out and challenging extremism. It is not about oppressing free speech or stifling academic freedom, it is about making sure that radical views and ideas are not given the oxygen they need to flourish. Schools, universities and colleges, more than anywhere else, have a duty to protect impressionable young minds and ensure that our young people are given every opportunity to reach their potential. That is what our one nation government is focused on delivering". The Prime Minister received regular updates from departments on how these proposals were being implemented to provide a comprehensive approach to dealing with extremism.[108]

The new legislation was certainly necessary. But the draft bill, while moving fractionally in the right direction, was seriously flawed. Government tried to bring its multitudinous powers together in a single bill. In this it has failed, with a number of important powers still

---

[107] The inquiry was prompted by the revelations from former CIA contractor turned whistleblower Edward Snowden, *The Guardian*, 12 March 2015
[108] Ibid.

lying outside the scope of the checks and oversights proposed under the draft legislation. The supposed strength of the new legislation was its "double lock" authorization process, with both ministerial and judicial approval required for the grant of any warrant. However, the decision to retain the home secretary's authorization process for domestic interception—the first lock of the double lock—is utterly irrational.[109]

Domestic interception should not be a political decision. In any event, this system does not offer any accountability, as Ministers never answered questions on security and certainly never admit to security errors. Even with surveillance powers other than domestic interception, the proposed "double lock" falls far short of what is needed, and fails to live up to government promises. Limiting judicial commissioners to considering warrants on judicial review principles means they can overrule a home secretary only if he or she is deemed to have acted utterly unreasonably. The government has hamstrung the process, in essence turning it into a judicial rubber stamp.

On 01 July 2015, Investigatory Powers Tribunal (IPT), which investigates complaints of unlawful contact by the UK intelligence agencies, notified Amnesty International that the British government agencies had spied on the organization by intercepting, accessing and storing its communications. The IPT previously identified one of two NGOs which it found had been subjected to unlawful surveillance by the UK government as the Egyptian Initiative for Personal Rights (EIPR), when it should have said Amnesty. The other NGO which was spied on was the Legal Resources Centre in South Africa. The UK surveillance agency GCHQ has been officially censured for not revealing enough about how it shares information with its American counterparts. The Investigatory Powers Tribunal said GCHQ failed until December 2014 to make clear enough details of how it shared data from mass Internet surveillance. It was the IPT's first ruling against an intelligence agency in its 15-year history. The Home Office said the government was "committed to transparency.[110]

In December the IPT ruled that the system of British intelligence collection did not breach the European Convention of Human Rights, following a complaint by campaign groups including Privacy International and Liberty. But the tribunal now ruled that the system

---

[109] Home Office Report, *the Telegraph* London, 04 June 2014
[110] Ibid.

did "contravene" human rights law-until extra information was made public in December. In its disclosures in December, GCHQ said British intelligence services were "permitted" to request information gathered by PRISM and UPSTREAM-US-surveillance-systems which can collect information on "non-US persons.[111]

All but one and half year inquiry by the intelligence and security committee of parliament (ISC) found that the existing laws are not being broken by the agencies and insisted that GCHQ's bulk interception does not amount to bulk surveillance. The inquiry was prompted by the revelations from former CIA contractor turned whistleblower Edward Snowden. The committee concluded that there was no bulk surveillance and gave a lengthy defense on it: "We have established that bulk interception cannot be used to search for and examine the communications of an individual in the UK unless GCHQ first obtain a specific authorization naming that individual, signed by a secretary of state."[112]

Extremist and radicalized elements continue to participate in overseas jihadist operations. Moreover, the PPPP strategy has also failed to intercept British jihadists from joining ISIS and Taliban networks. The scale of danger posed by extremists in and outside the country was underlined when jihadists threatened to kill non-Muslims in the streets of the UK. The returnees will be kept under surveillance as the government still looks for a community-based de-radicalization program. How will this be possible, given the government has never consulted the communities on counter-terrorism strategies and law enforcement mechanisms?

In addition, government is also thinking on different lines to restore control order. The idea of control order has already failed. Unless these extremist returnees are de-radicalized on the community level, no TERFOR or Control Order can intercept them from joining the ISIS terrorist network. Moreover, Britain also faces the threat of cyber terrorism. No doubt, the GCHQ is the best professional intelligence agency but we are unable to counter the threat of Chinese, Russian or Indian cyber-attacks as we still need to recruit young information warriors. They have established strong cyber forces respectively and use modern technologies of the kind we do not have. The UK Cyber Security Strategy (2011) also noted cyber threats coming from other

---

[111] The Crisis of Britain Surveillance state and also *the Guardian*, 01 August 2013
[112] Ibid.

states that seek to conduct espionage with the aim of spying on or compromising our government, military, industrial and economic assets, as well as monitoring opponents of their own regimes. The threat to national security has intensified as information warriors directly challenge us. The UK Home Office's recently noted: "A major cyber-attack on essential networks such as the national grid, police computers or supermarkets distribution systems could trigger severe social disruption."

Moreover, cyber-attacks that cause environmental and financial damage will carry a 14-year prison sentence. The irony is that we have failed to arrest a single cyber terrorist so far, while professional cyber warriors continue to establish their networks here and target state institutions. We are already facing a new kind of intelligence war in the UK that targets our institutions from a safe distance. We also face the threat of nuclear terrorism. Extremists and terrorists can gain access to nuclear materials like uranium and plutonium to make an improvised explosive device and use it against our critical infrastructure. In fact, the threat of the availability of nuclear material has intensified as technologies and capabilities proliferate. We can easily find ourselves in a far more dangerous world.

CHAPTER 5. REGULATIONS OF INVESTIGATORY POWER ACT 2000, AMERICAN AND BRITISH BULK SURVEILLANCE PROGRAMS AND COMMUNICATION INTERCEPTION

The Regulations of Investigatory Power Bill designed a policy and legal framework for law enforcement authorities, and gave unlimited powers of search, arrest, communication intercept, and privacy interference. In fact, this law authorized intelligence agencies to check what is going on in and outside the country, but it also received criticism from legal experts as they perceive it as a source of information gathering. This law reform the regime under which UK law enforcement bodies and intelligence agencies can be authorized by warrant to openly interfere in personal and collective communication, conduct interception, and retrieve information.

This reformed act also empowers Home Secretary to serve a data retention notice, directing a telecommunications operator to generate, obtain and retain communications data about users. Part 6 of the bill contains powers for the security and intelligence agencies to intercept communications, conduct equipment interference and to obtain communications data in bulk. Legal expert Graham Smith (2016) describes data retention regime and the power of the Secretary of State. He also called the act controversial and says some parts of the bill may face legal challenges:

> The existing compulsory data retention regime under the Data Retention and Investigatory Powers Act 2014 (DRIPA) expires at the end of December 2016. The parts of the Act that replace those provisions will have to be brought into effect before then. Existing

data retention notices issued under DRIPA or its predecessor legislation will continue automatically under the new Act up to 6 months without having to be reissued. At some point the Secretary of State can be expected to issue expanded data retention notices covering Internet connection records (site level browsing histories). However operators who receive such a notice are obliged not to disclose the existence or contents of the notice. Much of the Act is controversial. Some of it, particularly in the areas of bulk powers and data retention, is likely to be subject to legal challenge.[113]

In 2016, the commissioner who oversees interceptions by the security forces and local authorities allowed 517,236 permissions to look at communications data. The Guardian reported commissioner, Sir Anthony May, dismissed claims that there was "significant institutional overuse of communications data powers" However, Joanna Cavan, the head of the interception of communications commissioner's office (IOCCO), confirmed to the Guardian that inspections had found "breaches" in the way legally privileged material — private conversations between lawyers and their clients — had been handled by the intercepting agencies.[114]

The Guardian newspaper also reported some flaws in the interception process and quoted the report of the Interception Communication Commissioner who admitted sixty interception communication errors: "Sixty interception errors were reported. These ranged from over-collection and unauthorized selection or examination of material to the incorrect communications addresses being intercepted. Our inquiry into the retention, storage and deletion of intercepted material and data resulted in a significant amount of material and data being destroyed and retention periods being reduced as the interception agencies were not able to provide a persuasive justification to retain it." The Guardian reported.[115]

The law is considered as a strongest weapon against the anti state elements and those involved in terror acts. If we review the power of intelligence agencies, and their operational mechanism, we can find some flaws in their strategies. In spite the powers of intelligence agencies and law enforcement authorities, they failed to effectively

---

[113] The UK Investigatory Powers Act 2016 – what it will mean for your business, Graham Smith, Bird & Bird, 29 November 2016, https://www.twobirds.com/en/news/articles/2016/uk/what-the-investigatory-powers-bill-would-mean-for-your-business

[114] *The Guardian*, 12 March 2015

[115] Ibid.

counter terrorism and radicalization in the country. The 2017 terrorist attacks in Manchester and London proved the inability of the British intelligence to intercept terrorist elements. Every intelligence agency has strong and weak aspects; British intelligence also has so many weak points, which contradict its superpower status. Surveillance is the only tool British law enforcement agencies use against the citizens of the country. This tool is mostly used in Muslim dominated areas where radicalization and extremist challenge the authority of the police.

The backbone of British intelligence surveillance is TEMPORA that watch everyone with its changing sights, and collects every piece of intelligence information with care. This surveillance system has many eyes and ears that lesson to every social and political conversation across the country. In recent years, concern about the use of illegal surveillance by democratic, authoritarian and oppressive regimes is a clear violation of human rights. These exponentially growing concerns prompted the development of export control of surveillance technologies. In the United Kingdom, electronic approach to law enforcement and national security caused many challenges as the importance of human intelligence has been ignored. In all EU member states, communication meta-data is routinely gathered by telecom providers and Internet services providers to further the objectives of their businesses.

In all EU member states, various surveillance laws existed that define the retention period of data. Moreover, Cookies are another source of intelligence information that allow for faster navigation. Another way of information gathering is private surveillance technology firms that selling software application and tools used for interception communication purposes. Government and law enforcement agencies in EU member states are the main clients. The way information is collected and stored by cookies in EU is a queer way of information theft. On mass surveillance within member states, European Parliamentary Research Service in its 2015 paper defined the role of cookies in state information gathering process:

> Cookies allow for state management over the HTTP (Hypertext Transfer Protocol) protocol which is stateless by nature. In order to overcome this situation, the cookies were created as part of Internet standard to keep state information. Cookies are generated and modified by website servers, stored on client's local disks

and transmitted in every interaction between the server and the browser.[116] In terms of life-span, there are two main types of cookies: "Session cookies that are temporarily stored in memory and deleted once the connection session times out or when the browser is closed and second is persistent cookies that span over session and remain stored on the user's local desk, even when the browser is closed, until their expiration date. While session cookies purpose is to keep state information within sessions, persistent cookies are used for relating subsequent sessions or visit to a website.[117]

The introduction of mass surveillance law (2016) in Britain, and its complications forced government to clarify its stance. Recent revelations of US whistleblower Edward Snowden fueled tension between European states that already look at each other with suspicion. Germany cancelled its Cold War era pact with the UK while European intelligence agencies became more vigilant about the UK intelligence tactics. The National Security Agency (NSA) and the UK Government Communications Headquarters (GCHQ) had prepared a comprehensive list of individuals and institutions including the European competition commissioner, buildings and NGOs that provide financial assistance to Africa. Brussels reacted furiously to claim that the NSA and GCHQ spied on the European commissioner.[118]

The European commissioner has access to highly confidential commercial information. The commissioner's spokeswoman said, "This is not the type of behavior that we expect from strategic partners, let alone from our own member states."[119] Now, the EU decided to create its own intelligence agency by beginning the development of surveillance drones and spy satellites. The Italian Prime Minister attacked British Prime Minister David Cameron over allegations that the UK intercepted secret Italian communications and then passed them on to the NSA. The latest revelations from Edward Snowden show that the NSA and GCHQ spied on 100 top officials from 60 states, including the Israeli Prime Minister, European policy makers and several aid groups.[120]

---

[116] European Parliamentary Research Service paper-2015
[117] Ibid.
[118] The US and UK are members of the Five-Eye intelligence sharing alliance, including Australia, New Zealand and Canada, *Daily Times*, 07 January 2014
[119] *Huffington Post*, 20 December 2013
[120] The Crisis of Britain Surveillance State, Musa Khan Jalalzai, 2013

Britain maintains one of the world's most violent surveillance systems that spy on civilians and government officials day and night. Notwithstanding its operational mechanism, this spy machine has never been able to play a positive role in countering radicalization and extremism. The Machine's various tools are mostly installed in Muslim dominated areas, where government wants to spotlight extremist element and those terror suspects who are in search of an opportunity to carryout terror attacks against the government installations. These tools performance including CCTV's analysis techniques are very poor, relying on expensive cameras that always fail in facial recognition and tracking. In the UK seven police forces use surveillance technology that collects information from mobile phones. The hardware, known as an IMSI catcher, is a dangerous tool that locate phone user and intercept calls.

The UK citizens have no knowledge of the function of dozens secret intelligence units of their country. One of these secret units is an Electronic Intelligence Unit (EIU) that is responsible for surveillance; electronic propaganda campaign focuses on law enforcement mechanism and counter-terrorism operations. The Joint Threat Research Intelligence Group (JTRIG) is helping law enforcement agencies, including Met Police, MI5, Serious Organized Crime Agency (SOCA), Border Agency, Revenue and Customs (HMRC), and National Public Order and Intelligence Unit (NPOIU).[121] Researchers Glenn Greenwald and Andrew Fishman (22 June 2015) deeply analyzed the secret operational mechanism of this unit and elucidated many aspects of its revolving operational mechanism:

> Documents published by The Intercept demonstrate how the Joint Threat Research Intelligence Group (JTRIG), a unit of the signals intelligence agency Government Communications Headquarters (GCHQ), is involved in efforts against political groups it considers "extremist," Islamist activity in schools, the drug trade, online fraud and financial scams. Though its existence was secret until last year, JTRIG quickly developed a distinctive profile in the public understanding, after documents from NSA whistleblower Edward Snowden revealed that the unit had engaged in "dirty tricks" like deploying sexual "honey traps" designed to discredit targets, launching denial-of-service attacks to shut down Internet

---

[121] *Russian Television*, 29 June 2015

chat rooms, pushing veiled propaganda onto social networks and generally warping discourse online.[122]

On 13 June 2013, Washington Post and Guardian published important stories about the leaked information by Edward Snowden, which exposed the US and UK secret data gathering mechanism through PRISM, UPSTREAM and TEMPORA. After these revelations, simply, the UK intelligence committee declared that the allegations that GCHQ had acted illegally by accessing the content of private communications via the Prism program were "unfounded".[123] In 2015, the ISC conducted inquiry into the capabilities of electronic intelligence in intrusive techniques. The Intelligence Committee concluded that the existing legal framework governing these capabilities was unnecessarily complicated, and recommended that it be replaced with a new Act of Parliament.[124]

Edward Snowden in his TV interview in 2016 revealed that a new surveillance system operated by the US NSA and the UK GCHQ was called MUSCULAR. MUSCULAR is one of at least 4 other programs that rely on trusted program known as WINDSTOP. There were newspapers reports in 2012 and 2013, MUSCULAR collected 181 million records, while INCENSER collected 14 million records. The Washington Post report indicated that MUSCULAR program was strong in data collection than PRISM. MUSCULAR is free to collect data as much it want, and does not need warrants. Moreover, MUSCULAR also supporting the NSA's PINWALE surveillance system in data collection. On 09 February 2016, in his Daily Dot article, Eric Geller noted the power mechanism if GCHQ in data collection:

> GCHQ can collect "external" communications in bulk under a section 8(4) warrant. It can then search for and select communications to examine using a selector of an individual who is overseas, providing the Secretary of State has certified this as necessary for statutory purposes. If GCHQ wants to search for and select "external" communications to examine based on a selector of an individual in the UK, they must get additional authorization from a Secretary of State which names that person. The Secretary of State

---

[122] Controversial GCHQ Units Engaged in Domestic Law Enforcement, Online Propaganda, and Psychology Research, Glenn Greenwald and Andrew Fishman, 22 June 2015. https://theintercept.com/2015/06/22/controversial-gchq-unit-domestic-law-enforcement-propaganda/
[123] *Washington Post*, 13 June 2013, and also Intelligence Services: Key issues for the 2015 Parliament.
[124] Intelligence Services: Key issues for the 2015 Parliament

cannot issue section 8(1) or section 8(4) warrants unless they believe it is both necessary and proportionate.[125]

In January 2016, Reprieve, an international human rights organization reported members of the UK's Parliamentary intelligence watchdog will not be allowed access to all intelligence or defense information relating to the new British practice of targeted killing by drone. David Cameron was asked by Andrew Tyrie MP whether the Intelligence and Security Committee (ISC) would be allowed to examine the military aspect of the targeted killing programme, and whether he would commit to the Committee's security-cleared members being able to see all the relevant intelligence. Reprieve reported.[126] Mr. Cameron refused on both points, stating that the ISC's job was to examine intelligence, not military affairs, and that he could not give the commitment Mr. Tyrie asked for regarding the Committee's access to intelligence. Mr. Tyrie pointed out that what the Committee is allowed to see remains under the control of the Secretary of State, and that its work on targeted killing "could be rendered meaningless" if it were barred from looking at the military operation.[127]

The British government quietly re-wrote the law to permit its electronic intelligence agency to continue with controversial surveillance practices, according to campaigners. In a statement, Privacy International said: "The government has quietly ushered through legislation amending the anti-hacking laws to exempt GCHQ from prosecution. Privacy International and other parties were notified of these just hours prior to a hearing of their claim against GCHQ's illegal hacking operations in the Investigatory Powers Tribunal."[128]

Since the first reporting on documents disclosed by Edward Snowden in June 2013, a number of challenges to GCHQ's surveillance practices have been initiated in the UK. In response to one of those applications, from Liberty and several other organizations, the court that oversees the GCHQ ruled against the UK intelligence services for the first time in its controversial 15 year history. In the short, two-page ruling, the Investigatory Powers Tribunal declared that, before

---

[125] Eric Geller, *Daily Dot*, 09 February 2016
[126] *Reprieve* (international human rights organization) report, 12 January 2016
[127] Ibid.
[128] *Wall Street Journal*, 07 January 2016

December 2014 "the regime governing the soliciting, receiving, storing and transmitting by the UK authorities of private communications of individuals in the UK, which have been obtained by the US authorities"[129] under the NSA's PRISM and UPSTREAM (collection from fiber-optic cable) programs breached Articles 8 and 10 of the European Convention on Human Rights.[130]

These illegal interventions of the US and UK governments in the privacy of European states created a climate of mistrust across the continent, while Germany strongly protested against the UK spying on its institutions. In the UK, parliamentarians and politicians expressed deep concern over the complaints of European leaders against the UK's intelligence politics. In 2014, the three chiefs of the intelligence agencies—MI5, MI6, and GCHQ—appeared before the Intelligence and Security Committee to explain the way intelligence operates. The US and UK are members of the Five-Eye intelligence sharing alliance, including Australia, New Zealand and Canada, but their method of surveillance clearly violates the principles of the alliance. French intelligence is cooperating with the Five Eyes alliance by systematically providing them with information. Sweden, Israel and Italy are also cooperating with the NSA and GCHQ.[131]

The Intelligence and Security Committee (ISC) was established in 1994, to oversee the expenditures of MI5, MI6 and GCHQ. It was reformed through the Justice and Intelligence Act 2013. Normally, national oversight practices vary greatly in term of how much power is granted to intelligence services, and how they are accountable for their actions. In most European states, democratic accountability of intelligence agencies is of great importance. Executive control, parliamentary oversight, judicial review, internal control and independent scrutiny are the ways democratic accountability is ensured.[132] As a multicultural society, Britain has established a wide-ranging intelligence infrastructure to tackle extremism and international terrorism. Over the past forty years, specifically, technological advancement confined human being to limited activities. With this advancement, the power of the state also increased to carry out surveillance upon its citizens.

---

[129] *The Guardian* 05 February 2015
[130] *Privacy International*, 09 June 2016
[131] *Daily Times*, 07 January 2014
[132] Ibid.

Knowledge and surveillance management compared to policing policy, has received surprisingly considerable attention. Intelligence has always been of much importance for security and law enforcement agencies. With the introduction of Special Arish Branch in 1883, the work of intelligence has been central in the operations of many police operational units in the country. Intelligence is a well-classified, analyzed and processed knowledge, which plays important role in the preparation of security plans of a state. Intelligence is knowledge, a decision oriented and action oriented knowledge. Without decision oriented knowledge and action oriented knowledge, no knowledge and information can help security agencies in the protection of state security.

Having provided accurate analytical information to the state and government, intelligence pinpoints the level of internal and external threats. Secret agencies (MI5 and MI6, GCHQ, DIS, JIC, CID, NIM, BI, Special Branch) in Britain have a brilliant intelligence record of over one hundred years. Special Branch, that played important role in the first and second world wars, was established in 1883. There are three other important intelligence agencies in the United Kingdom, known as MI5, MI6 and GCHQ, protecting the national security of the country. All these agencies are working under Intelligence Act 1994, Security Service Acts 1989 and 1996. Established in 1909, MI6 is working as foreign intelligence, responsible to the foreign office of the country. MI6 gather information overseas. Another well reputed secret service, MI5, established in 1909, is operating under the 1994 Intelligence Act, working closely with the local police.[133]

In February 2017, some members of an intellectual gathering in London said that Britain's intelligence agencies cannot do their job without the consent of their masters. Their hands are tied with Ministerial rope. Richard M. Bennett and Katie Bennett in their well-written report on British intelligence revealed some important facts about their accountability and responsibility: "Britain has a complicated and rather bureaucratic political control over its intelligence and security community and one that tends to apply itself to long term targets and strategic intelligence program, but has little real influence on the behavior and operations of SIS and MI5. Not so much 'oversight' as blind-sight. Despite the domestic changes

---

[133] House of Commons, 05 July 2016, Intelligence and Security Committee of Parliament Annual Report 2015-2016

of recent years and their formal establishment as legal government organizations, there is still little true accountability for their action or valid test of their overall efficiency".[134]

This myriad of organizations include the four main elements of the UK intelligence community; Secret Intelligence Service (MI6) responsible for foreign intelligence, the Security Service (MI5), responsible for internal security and counter espionage within both the UK and Commonwealth countries. The GCHQ, Government Communication Headquarters, SIGINT and COMSEC agency and the DIS, Defense Intelligence Staff, responsible for the intelligence and security activities within the UK armed forces. They report to the JIC and through then to the civil Service (PSIS) and finally the Ministerial Committee (MIS).[135]

However, the issue of interception communication has become more complicated as complaints came from various circles about their privacy and family life. The law of surveillance is being amended time and again, but in spite of all these technological efforts, no specific progress has been made in the interception of extremist's e-mails entering the country. The law of terror or the Regulation of Investigatory Power Act 2000 (RIPA), Communication Act 1985 and the Police Act 1997, allow the state security agencies to intercept communications. On 16 June 2013, daily Guardian published a comprehensive report about the role of British intelligence agencies in interception communication which revealed that agencies not only set up fake Internet cafes to secure information on diplomats while RIPA allowed agencies to use all ways of information collection:

> The powers that allow British's intelligence agencies to spy on individuals, including foreign diplomats, were set out in the 1994 Intelligence Services Act (ISA). They were framed in a broad way to allow those involved in espionage to conduct all manner of operations with ministerial authority, and the type of technique used during the G20 summit four years ago suggest a creativity and technological capability.[136] After GCHQ, MI5 and MI6 were given their remit through the ISA; the Regulation of Investigatory Powers Act (RIPA) gave the agencies more precise tools to gather intelligence through techniques such as targeted interceptions. Under RIPA, the director general of MI5, the Chief of MI6 and the Director of GCHQ

---

[134] Espionage: Spies and Secrets, Richard Bennett, Random House, 24 Apr 2012
[135] The UK Intelligence and Security Report, August 2003, Richard M. Bennett and Katie Bennett, AFI Research
[136] *The Guardian* 16 June 2013

are among 10 very senior officials who can apply for warrant to either the foreign or home secretary.[137]

Interception of communication in the United Kingdom has been central in media and intellectual forums since 2001. There have been many complaints in public and government circles regarding the phone tapping, bugging, e-mail hacking and privacy violation, but according to the Regulation of Investigatory Power Act 2000 (RIPA) and, specifically, Interception Communication Act, police and intelligence agencies have legal authority to intercept communication. Orla Lynskey has described the legal control of data sharing with the United States and elucidates the legal aspects of privacy of British citizens in her recent article:

> Following the revelation that US intelligence agencies are engaged in widespread surveillance of Internet communications using the so called 'PRISM' program, President Obama's guarantees that PRISM does not apply to US citizens and it does not apply to people living in the US is unlikely to reassure many of this side of the Atlantic. PRISM gives the US National Security Agency (NSA) access to both communications contents and traffic data held of servers of global Internet communications heavyweights such as Google, Face book and Apple. The PRISM revelation quickly led to the concern that the UK's Government Communications Headquarter (GCHQ) was gathering data on UK citizens via PRISM thereby circumventing the protection offered by the UK legal framework. William Hague, appearing before the commons, was quick to refute this claim describing it as 'baseless.[138]

According to the RIPA's section 12, Secretary of State can authorize the relevant authority on the issue of interception. However, some people including parliamentarians recorded complaints regarding their telephone monitoring, but there are some laws that allow monitoring the telephone calls. Some laws that authorize state security agencies for monitoring are, Regulation of the Investigatory Power Act 2000 (RIPA), Telecommunications Interception Act of 2000 (TIA), Data Protection Act 1998 (DPA), and Telecommunication Regulations of 1999.[139]

---

[137] Ibid.
[138] Looking through a legal PRISM at UK and US intelligence agency surveillance, Orla Lynskey, http://blogs.lse.ac.uk/politicsandpolicy/looking-through-a-legal-prism-at-uk-and-us-intelligence-agency-surveillance/
[139] *The Crisis of Britain's Surveillance State*, Musa Khan Jalalzai, 2014

In the Annual Report (2012) of Interception Communications Commissioner, (ICC) presented to Parliament pursuant to section 58 (6) of the Regulation of Investigatory Power Act 2000, it has been suggested that media and public still needs to understand RIPA and the way it defines the remit of the commissioner, the Lawful Interception of Communication and the Acquisition of Communications Data (LICACD). Part-1, Chapter 2 of RIPA provides the power to acquire communications data. The RIPA bill was introduced in the House of Commons on 9 February 2000 and completed its parliamentary passage on 26 July.[140]

RIPA regulates the manner in which certain public bodies may conduct surveillance and access a person's electronic communications. The role of Interception Communications Commissioner has been defined in RIPA. Interception and communication has been long established practice in the UK, but before 1985, there was no specific law or framework. Ordinances had been governing the practice. From 1957 to 1981; government in the United Kingdom had three official reports available to the public. These reports were the 1957 Becket Report, the 1980 White Paper and the 1981 Dip lock Report. In 1985, government hinted about the introduction of Interception Communications Act. Later on, following the White Paper, the same year, Interception of Communication Act was introduced.[141]

In addition to this, the Government established more joint intelligence working groups to tackle the issue of terrorism technically. Joint Terrorism Analysis Centre, Centre for the Protection of National Infrastructure, Joint Intelligence Committee and Assessment Staff and IT centre under the supervision of GCHQ. All these institutions play very important role in tackling violent extremism and criminal culture in the country. Intelligence and Security Committee in its report has given much importance to the analysis and responsibilities of the Defense Intelligence Staff (DIS):

The defense intelligence staffs (DIS) is a critical part of the country intelligence community, and a single largest intelligence analytical capability in the UK." Home Office in its study report has claimed that Internet protocol based communications will render the UK's domestic interception capabilities obsolete over the next decade. However, the Home Secretary told the committee: "We do recognize

---

[140] Ibid.
[141] Ibid.

the changing technology that we are facing, the way in which both the collection and dissemination of information Britain's National Security Challenges and data will change fundamentally, and it will change more quickly in this country then it will in many others . . .The impact of that will be to massively degrade (unless we make big changes) out ability, not just to be able to intercept, but actually potentially to be able to collect the communications data in the first place in order to be able to target the interception.[142]

Today, citizens of Britain are facing the worst form of cyber terrorism. Cyber warriors use electronic attacks on institutions for many advantages. First, it is cheaper and the action is very difficult to be tracked. Second, they also use the method of distributed denial of services to overburden the government and its agencies electronic bases. A recent detailed investigation of the Indian government revealed that a cyber spy network is operating out of China, which is targeting the Indian business, diplomatic, strategic and academic interests. India complains about Pakistan's cyber-attacks as well. However, cyber war between Iran and the Arab world is another interesting story. Iranian hackers have been trying to retrieve sensitive data from the computers of state institutions of various Arab states since long. To destroy Iranian nuclear program, Israel sends strong viruses to the computers of Iranian nuclear installations.

---

[142] *The Telegraph*, 07 February 2009

Chapter 6. The Snoopers' Charter Surveillance 2016: Unchallengeable Power to Hack Government and Private Computers

The Investigatory Powers Bill was introduced by Home Secretary Theresa May. The bill legitimized the security services' surveillance powers while adding checks on their ability to gather information about citizens without a warrant.[143] In its Summary note of the Investigatory Powers Act 2016, the UK Parliament on its website argued: "A Bill to make provision about the interception of communications, equipment interference and the acquisition and retention of communications data, bulk personal datasets and other information; to make provision about the treatment of material held as a result of such interception, equipment interference or acquisition or retention; to establish the Investigatory Powers Commissioner and other Judicial Commissioners and make provision about them and other oversight arrangements; to make further provision about investigatory powers and national security; to amend sections 3 and 5 of the Intelligence Services Act 1994; and for connected purposes".[144]

On 29 November 2016, the Investigatory Power Bill became the "Power Act" after receiving royal assent. The Act sets three important duties and responsibilities. The Act:

---

[143] *The Telegraph*, London, 29 November 2016, http://www.telegraph.co.uk/technology/2016/11/29/investigatory-powers-bill-does-mean-privacy/
[144] Investigatory Powers Act 2016, the UK Parliament Website, http://services.parliament.uk/bills/2015-16/investigatorypowers.html

...brings together all of the powers already available to law enforcement and the security and intelligence agencies to obtain communications and data about communications. It will make these powers and the safeguards that apply to them clear and understandable. Radically overhauls the way these powers are authorized and overseen. It introduces a 'double-lock' for interception warrants, so that, following Secretary of State Authorization, these (and other warrants) cannot come into force until they have been approved by a judge. And it creates a powerful new Investigatory Powers Commissioner to oversee how these powers are used, and ensures powers are fit for the digital age. It makes provision for the retention of Internet connection records for law enforcement to identify the communications service to which a device has connected. This will restore capabilities that have been lost as a result of changes in the way people communicate.[145]

Intelligence and surveillance experts have categorically concluded that offensive surveillance and illegal interference in private lives of citizens can alienate them from the state. They believe that electronic approach to national security and law enforcement has never been a proper panacea to the fear and insecurity of civilian population. The new law has crossed all limits of human rights and privacy that gazes at civilians in an offensive mode. We must understand that laws like this cannot bring stability to the state and cannot protect us from the wrath of foreign espionage, lone wolves and violent radicalized groups.

Face Book, Google, YouTube and other spying agencies those collect a significant amount of user data to make stronger state agencies in their espionage campaign against the privacy of innocent civilians have been in deep water after the Edwards Joseph Snowden's revelations about the US surveillance mechanism. In the past, British state acted clandestinely used unwritten prerogative powers of opening emails and tapping telephones calls. In the Netherlands, Germany, and Brussels, France and in the UK, intelligence surveillance has generated new debates that as the state agencies have failed to demonstrate professionally in countering terrorism and domestic radicalization; they resorted to the use of violent surveillance mechanism against their civilians.

---

[145] Investigatory Powers Act, Home Office Published in March 2016, last updated: 23 February 2017. https://www.gov.uk/government/collections/investigatory-powers-bill

Intelligence role in national security and law enforcement has always received greater importance in all EU member states. As we mentioned earlier, that in every member state, intelligence agencies have different priorities and legal boundaries. Electronic intelligence in the EU falls within the domain of the member state that have sole responsibilities to tackle the issues of internal security. On 06 September 2015, Library of Congress in its report on foreign intelligence mechanism defined the operational mechanism of intelligence surveillance in European Union:

> Electronic surveillance conducted by national law enforcement authorities is inherently linked to the right to privacy and personal data protection. Such rights are enshrined in European Union treaties and secondary legislation as well as in conventions adopted by the council of Europe and in the international convection on civil and political rights, which binds EU members. The charter of fundamental rights and the European convention for the Protection of Human Rights and Fundamental Freedom guarantee the right to privacy and personal data protection to everyone within the jurisdiction of the EU member states. Legal issues arising from electronic surveillance that may infringe in the human rights of individuals are not subject to review by the court of justice of the EU... Following the Snowden revelations in the United States and press reports of mass electronic surveillance conducted by law enforcement authorities of several EU Members, the European Parliament adopted a resolution on the US NSA Surveillance Programme, Surveillance Bodies in various (EU) Members States and Their Impact on EU Citizen's Fundamental Rights.[146]

The introduction of new mass surveillance law in Britain is a sign of deteriorating security, and law and order situation that has become a permanent torment for the UK Home Office and law enforcement infrastructure. The UK is under threat from internal and external forces and needs a professional approach to national security to tackle the exponentially growing Talibanization, radicalization, extremism, and international terrorism. The new surveillance law gives the country's secret agencies the most sweeping powers, not a long-term panacea to the above mentioned diseases.

The Investigatory Powers Act legalized the whole range of tools for snooping and hacking business of British intelligence agencies, which generated a countrywide debate in print and electronic media.

---

[146] Library of Congress Report, 06 September 2015

The report of Intelligence Services Commissioner for 2015 elucidated the role of intelligence agencies in retention of Bulk Personal Dataset by any means. Section 2(2)(a) of the Security Service Act 1989, section 2(2)(a) and 4(2)(a) of the Intelligence Services Act 1994, also known as the "information gateway provisions", and section 19 of the Counter-Terrorism Act 2008 allow for the agencies to acquire and retain Bulk Personal Datasets (BPDs) overtly or covertly.[147]

The chain of surveillance and uncontrollable secret watchdog activities is not the proper panacea for deteriorating security. The reason is that intelligence and policing agencies have failed to counter cyber-attacks or terrorist networks and cells operating across the country. With the GCHQ becoming more powerful, we need to know more about the actual function of the agency and its specter of surveillance mechanism. We also need to know how powerful GCHQ is and what is the range of its surveillance. We need to know about the agency operations through the recent, complicated and strong surveillance law promulgated in Britain. The agency has legal powers to hack, intercept and block our emails, messages, phone calls, and computer communications networks. GCHQ today is quite different from the NSA, and to some extent a powerful, accurate and reliable agency, but one thing is clear that the lawmakers mostly consider that the agency is a security umbrella of Britain that counters every destabilizing element inside the country.[148]

The UK police and intelligence agencies were given full power to hack into private computer without the permission of information and intelligence commissioners. The law was deeply criticized by human rights groups that this would undermine the privacy of computer users. This controversial law was declared by European highest court illegal, but newspapers reported that agencies still use those powers, which are against basic human rights. Garry Crystal spotlighted important aspects of the law in his article:

> There are number of ways that the police can hack into a personal computer without the user's knowledge. Remote searching means that the police can hack into the user's computer from another location. This is achieved by sending a virus to the suspect's computer in an email. The police would then be able to view the suspect's emails and browsing habits. Key logging is another form

---

[147] Intelligence Services commissioner Office website details, 23 January 2016
[148] *Daily Times*, 29 November 2016

of hacking that send back details of each keyboard key used by the suspect and can be used to obtain passwords. Wireless networking can be used to hack into a suspect's computer and monitor their online activities and search hard drives.[149]

The new surveillance law gives more unchallengeable power to secret agencies, while the Investigatory Power Bill wants websites to keep customer's browsing history for up to one year and allow agencies the right of access to data while investigating a case. Edward Snowden already mentioned these apprehensions in his recent tweeted message: "The UK has just legalized the most extreme surveillance in the history of western democracy. It goes further than many autocracies." However, on 17 October 2016, the Investigatory Power Tribunal, the court that hears complaints against MI6, MI5 and GCHQ, ruled that these agencies had been unlawfully collecting massive volumes of confidential personal data without proper oversight for 17 years. Now, as the cat is out of the bag, and the 17 years' practices have become legalized, the TEMPORA will continue to watch us by all means.

Human rights and privacy groups challenged the law in the EU Court of Justice.

> The passage of the Snoopers' Charter through parliament is a sad day for British liberty. Under the guise of counter-terrorism, the state has achieved totalitarian-style surveillance powers the most intrusive system of any democracy in human history," said a human rights activist. Open Rights Director, Jim Killock said, "The UK has now a surveillance law that is more suited to a dictatorship than a democracy. The state has unprecedented powers to monitor and analyses UK citizen's communications regardless of whether we are suspected of any criminal activity."[150]Chief Executive of Big Brother Watch groups, Renate Samson warned, "The passing of the investigatory power bill has fundamentally changed the face of surveillance in this country. None of us online are now guaranteed the right to communicate privately, and most importantly, securely.[151]

The revelations of Edward Joseph Snowden about the UK mass surveillance system transformed our understanding of how our most advanced and professional electronic intelligence agency (GCHQ)

---

[149] Police computer hacking powers and civil liberties, Garry Crystal, Civil Rights Movement, 21 December 2016 http://www.civilrightsmovement.co.uk/police-computer-hacking-powers-civil-liberties.html
[150] Ibid.
[151] *Daily Times*, 29 November 2016

monitor us through its surveillance system day and night. Mr. Snowden unveiled a range of different tactics by which our security agencies collect and analyze Internet communication metadata. Perceptions of technicalities in law enforcement mechanism must be clear when dealing with national security issues by electronic means. If we ultimately depend on surveillance or electronic means of controlling the persistent unspecified population and its evolving perceptions of a peaceful society, we would not be able to counter the looming national security threats.

In this globalized world, CCTV camera, helicopter, car, drone and many other means of electronic surveillance cannot paint a positive picture of law and order management, nor can we through them truly perceive a peaceful society. It is our fundamental right to know how Regulations of Investigatory Power Act-2000 (RIPA) and law enforcement agencies implement laws and what mechanism is adopted. Mr. Snowden in his recent revelations elucidated the scope of surveillance through TEMPORA and the use of warrants for the interception of communications under section 8 (4) of RIPA.

Conventional wisdom asks whether this new trail of surveillance measures will ensure our peace of mind, physical security of our children and business, or will it further embroil our society in a multi-faceted crisis? The answer is not clear, but it is an irrevocable fact that at present, we are living in a climate of fear due to the arrival of newly trained terror and criminal elements in our streets and markets that make things worse with their activities ranging from drug to human trafficking, and from espionage to terror-related businesses. Criminal gangs are making millions and terror elements receiving money from the UK based radicalized groups before carrying out attacks against government installations and public businesses, and this can be seen as the high graph of target killings. Now the question is where haw effective is the snooper charter surveillance against these elements?

The Investigatory Powers Bill 2016 demarcated the legal boundaries of the electronic surveillance powers of the UK Intelligence Community and police. In November 2015, the draft bill was published with a slew of related documents.

In 2016, the House of Commons and the House of Lords passed the bill providing a clear and transparent basis for the powers already in use by the security and intelligence services.

Authorities allowed to access Internet connection records:

Metropolitan police force
City of London police force
Police forces maintained under section 2 of the Police Act 1996
Police Service of Scotland
Police Service of Northern Ireland
British Transport Police
Ministry of Defense Police
Royal Navy Police
Royal Military Police
Royal Air Force Police
Security Service
Secret Intelligence Service
GCHQ
Ministry of Defense
Department of Health
Home Office
Ministry of Justice
National Crime Agency
HM Revenue & Customs
Department for Transport
Department for Work and Pensions
NHS trusts and foundation trusts in England that provide ambulance services
Common Services Agency for the Scottish Health Service
Competition and Markets Authority
Criminal Cases Review Commission
Department for Communities in Northern Ireland
Department for the Economy in Northern Ireland
Department of Justice in Northern Ireland
Financial Conduct Authority
Fire and rescue authorities under the Fire and Rescue Services Act 2004
Food Standards Agency
Food Standards Scotland
Gambling Commission
Gang masters and Labor Abuse Authority
Health and Safety Executive
Independent Police Complaints Commissioner
Information Commissioner
NHS Business Services Authority
Northern Ireland Ambulance Service Health and Social Care Trust
Northern Ireland Fire and Rescue Service Board
Northern Ireland Health and Social Care Regional Business Services
    Organization
Office of Communications

Office of the Police Ombudsman for Northern Ireland
Police Investigations and Review Commissioner
Scottish Ambulance Service Board
Scottish Criminal Cases Review Commission
Serious Fraud Office
Welsh Ambulance Services National Health Service Trust[152]

Every year, we are saddled with a new bunch surveillance and immigration laws, policing security measures, and terror-related acts and ordinances, but this load of legal restrictions never adds up to a long-term solution. Every month, the police department issues new guidance to the communities for the safety and security of their children and houses, but criminal and radicalized elements do not bother with this instruction; they are free to harass and terrorize communities with impunity. The ooze remains, and we are still in a state of fear, while individual and group terrorists still remain a threat, and the fear of the return of ISIS recruited elements from Iraq and Syria. We want the UK intelligence agencies to improve their operational mechanism and counter terrorism capacity to prevent radicalized elements from entering the country.

The war of intelligence also started between European states and the UK when France, Germany and Spain summoned both the UK and US ambassadors to explain their motive behind surveillance politics. Because offensive surveillance measures, they use in their own states cannot be applied on Europe. Germany hammered UK when it found that the Berlin-based UK embassy was involved in alleged eavesdropping. The revelations by Mr. Snowden also sparked widespread outrage not only in Germany but also created an alarming situation in other European states. With this, the intelligence war of all euro-state started in UK soil as we have already experienced the arrest of several foreign spies in the past. A government security document published in The Daily Telegraph warned that the UK is a high priority target for 20 foreign intelligence agencies. Intelligence reports revealed that Iranian, Korean, Serbian and Syrian intelligence agencies have roots in UK society while the intelligence agencies of Pakistan, India, Bangladesh and some European states, such as France and Germany, also presence in the field.[153]

---

[152] Owen Hughes, *International Business Times*, November 28, 2016
[153] *Weekly the Nation*, 02 December 2016

History tells us that the EU represents strong and well-resources nations of the first and second world wars, which share poverty, unemployment and homelessness with each other. The Security Service, on its website, has warned about the vulnerability of institutions to foreign intelligence agencies: "The UK is a high priority espionage target. Many countries actively seek UK information and material to advance their own military, technological, political and economic program". The activities of intelligence agencies identified as posing the greatest threat are subject to particular scrutiny. The threat against British interests is not confined to within the UK itself. A foreign intelligence service operates best in its own country and therefore finds it easier to target UK interests at home, where they can control the environment and take advantage of any perceived vulnerabilities.

The Sunday Telegraph reported Whitehall's concern about the foreign spying network in the UK. According to the newspaper report, Britain's European neighbors, including Germany and France, were also engaged in industrial and political espionage within the UK. Diplomatic ruction between the UK and other European states over intelligence surveillance has now caused mistrust as they blame each other for spying on their citizens and leaders. The flames of this conflagration are now felt in the UK and can ignite the violent fire of a crucial intelligence war on the country's soil. In this possible war, the UK might face an uneven situation if the European intelligence infrastructure entered into revenge politics. In the near future, this intelligence war may make the UK more vulnerable to hostile secret networks. The police may face an uncontrollable situation in tackling serious organized crime, and intelligence agencies will be in trouble countering expected invisible forces.[154]

UK law enforcement is in deep crisis. One can understand the fear and irritation of law enforcement agencies when they know that terrorist and espionage networks are making trouble across the country despite all efforts to knock them out. In November 2012, during the election of the police and crime commissioner, the anti-privatization campaign received strong support.

Recently, the head of counter terrorism in the Metropolitan Police Department, Mark Rowley, appealed to the public for help in identifying jihadis and potential terrorists in communities. Terror-

---

[154] *Weekly the Nation*, 02 December 2016

related incidents have increased fivefold. "The growth of dangerous individuals poses challenges for policing, especially when nearly half of Syria travelers of concern were not known as terrorist risks previously," Rowley revealed. Ethnic minorities are needed in the police force in order to reach out to the populace, yet figures released under the Freedom of Information Act show that ethnic minority representation is low. Newly published data show that 32 of the country's 45 territorial police forces appoint a disproportionate number of white people.

The CIA alone produced more than 1,000 malware system viruses, Trojan and other software that can infiltrate and take control of targeted devices, according to a document released by Wikileaks as reported by Al Jazeera on 07 March 2017. This is the output of the CIA's 200-strong Center for Cyber Intelligence; it shows the abilities of its hackers. (This was among the 9,000 secret files that were the first tranche of documents released by Wikileaks in March 2017.[155])

Cyber security organizations are desperately seeking ways to respond while private firms are looking towards the most trusted intelligence agency, the Government Communication Headquarters (GCHQ) to take action. As we are being told about the sensitivity of this violent security threat, our intelligence agencies are also restive and anxious about the day-to-day changing mechanism of cyber terrorist groups.

The country's Emergency Response Team (ERT) is failing. As part of a £ 650 million government investment in countering cyber terrorism, the unit has the core responsibility to respond to the looming threat of economic crimes. Experts have warned time and again that cyber criminals from around the world are using sophisticated technologies to steal important data.[156]

Government agencies are being attacked up to 33,000 times a month by cyber terrorist networks. The GCHQ told the media that the agency was struggling to recruit more cyber security experts as the country was at risk of being "left behind and at a disadvantage globally." The UK has also asked why the Five Eyes intelligence alliance has not addressed this threat effectively? Every year, the

---

[155] On 07 March 2017, *Al Jazeera* reported *Wikileaks* revealed that the document it released show the CIA produced more than 1,000 malware system-viruses, Trojan and other software that can infiltrate and take control of targeted electronics
[156] *The Guardian* 25 March 2016

Cameron government highlighted cyber terrorism as a priority alongside international terrorism, but they still lack the necessary technology. When the crisis deepened, former Prime Minister David Cameron announced more than £ 1.1 billion investment in a military program to tackle these modern threats posed by global terrorism and economic jihadists. This money could mostly be used to pay for new hi-tech surveillance and intelligence gathering equipment.

In 2013, NATO published a 330-page report that prompted a reaction from Russia. The document was called 'Tallinn Manual of Cyber Warfare.' The manual's biggest section is devoted to cyber-attacks that accompany traditional armed conflicts.[157]

In March 2014, NATO and its allies experienced cyber-attacks on a large scale while the Syrian Electronic Army (SEA) announced on Twitter that it had successfully hacked into the networks of CENTCOM that oversees US military operations from Turkey to Afghanistan, as well as the Pacific Command. In Afghanistan, underground cyber strategic commands established strong networks and retrieved the US, NATO, UK and ISAF's military and operational plans through their cyber warriors easily. They trained their partners who worked for them and purveyed top secret military and intelligence information to their cyber commands.

The Royal Air Force (RAF) MENWITH Hill is a US and UK secret intelligence information gathering/surveillance system, jointly operated by the RAF and NSA. This is the most secret and important intelligence surveillance agency outside the United States.[158] The importance of MENWITH Hill cannot be ignored in the information and intelligence surveillance game. It covers all aspects of intercepting communications and strategic movements across Asia and Europe. Operating since 1960s, MENWITH Hill is a highly professional and competent intelligence surveillance system that gathers information through its advanced technologies. This system is responsible for Signal Intelligence (SIGINT) and is an integral part of Global network. The MENWITH Hill surveillance system also has responsibility of interception of business-related and commercial transmissions from other nation's satellites.[159]

---

[157] Ibid.
[158] *Independent*, 24 January 2014
[159] *The Guardian*, 01 March 2012

MENWITH Hill was kept secret for many years by both the US and UK government, but some Western journalists reached its sites and retrieved information about it. Over the last 50 years, American secret agencies have been secretly constructing an enormous electronic spy station in Yorkshire (UK). Notwithstanding the end of the cold war, Pentagon, CIA and NSA continue to spy on their allies and enemies overtly and covertly. Over the years, the relationship between the NSA and GCHQ became clearer, as the intelligence sharing process strengthened and representatives of GCHQ were stationed inside the MENWITH Hill headquarters.

For years, experts and researchers were in tense struggle to find true information about this secret system, while human rights groups were actively seeking transparency about its operations, but policy makers in London have often refused to provide information about the role of MENWITH Hill in national security. Recently, a top secret document obtained by Intercept offered good information about this system. Over the last ten years, NSA had been secretly running new spying system with names such as GHOSTHUNTER and GHOSTWOLF, which supported the UK and US military operations against al Qaeda in Afghanistan and Iraq. Moreover, another spy satellite was operating in 2009 from MENWITH Hill for intercepting communications. However, to identify Internet cafes across Middle East and Africa supporting US operations against terrorism in the region, GHOSTHUNTER was in full operation in 2009 that geo-located more than 5,000 Very Small Aperture Terminals (VSAT) as a satellite system used by governments in the region.[160]

In 2017, the Defense Ministry of Russia planned to complete the formation of a special cyber security force designed to protect its armed forces' networks. This plan is a part of the country's program to modernize its information security. A report from Moscow also revealed that Russian military forces were planning to begin setting up cyber warfare forces for both defense and cyber-attacks. The command of this force will be headed by an army general. The Russian media continues to publish news stories about the digitization of the country's armed forces to compete with US and NATO allies' forces in Asia and Europe. Their need for a cyber defense shield has been

---

[160] Ibid.

prompted by the armed forces' transition to new types of weapons with a high share of digital components.[161]

The Russian government has hinted about the future of its cyber defense force. According to recent reports in the Russian media, this defense force will have different levels of technical, cryptographic and radio-electronic security duplicating each other and protecting strategic defense facilities. The information warfare between the West and Russia is not new, and even between Washington and its allies. Attacks on state computers in all directions have been routine for a long time, but lately there has been a desire to form a collective cyber strategy on the European level to counter cyber-attacks. In the UK there is a professional infrastructure in place, but we still need to improve the GCHQ's capabilities in countering cyber terrorist attacks. The information war is modern war, and Russia, India and China are considered to be in strong positions — possibly the strongest.

In recent years, cyber-attacks have deeply endangered state institutions around the world, but states in the European continent have realized the importance of cyber security strategy in protecting national critical infrastructure. The United States, EU and the UK government issue statements, but in reality they have developed no consensus to effectively respond to their rivals.

The security environment is changing; law and order are giving way to chaos and insecurity. Law enforcement agencies have failed to control more than 3,000 criminal gangs. The threat of terrorism is constant and the fight against extremists continues, while international gangs run greater and greater smuggling operations, trafficking in everything from drugs and weapons to victims of kidnapping. There are more than 90,000 criminals selling narcotics on the streets and in schools and colleges of the country.

Meanwhile, "for our security" the state has installed more and more cameras in public areas. The overwhelming intrusion into people's personal lives has caused a breakdown in trust between the citizens and the state. Five Eyes (the intelligence alliance between Britain, the US, Australia, Canada and New Zealand), TEMPORA, PRISM, ECHELON and the politics of the intelligence war in cyberspace have shaken the public perception that their governments respect civil rights and liberties.

---

[161] Ibid.

The year 2017 continues to give us more information about the ongoing violence in Northern Ireland where the political parties failed to agree on a power sharing formula after the Good Friday Agreement, and illicit trade in drugs and nuclear materials in Central and South Asia have further jeopardized the national security of the state. The September 2014 referendum in Scotland also became a challenging problem. The performance of several state institutions raised many questions as countless scandals smeared their reputation. The banks lost the trust of both the public and government as a result of their incompetence. Now, British citizens ask, where does the country place itself at this stage of deep crisis and instability?[162]

Recent developments in cyber technology have highlighted the intensity of information war among states through non-state actors or their own military forces. These developments are, notably, a good progress in modernizing national armies in Asia and Europe, but it also put in danger the security of small states. In their research paper on Cyber Warfare for the Congressional Research Service (2015), Catherine A Theohary and John W. Rollins have defined the basic concept and function of cyber warfare and cyber terrorism:

> Cyber war is typically conceptualized as state-on-state action equivalent to an armed attack or use of force in cyberspace that may trigger a military response with a proportional kinetic use of force. Cyber terrorism can be considered "the premeditated use of disruptive activities, or the threat thereof, against computer and/ or networks, with the intension to cause harm of further social, ideological religious, political or similar objectives, or to intimidate ant person in furtherance of such objectives." Cybercrime include unauthorized network breaches and theft of intellectual property and other data; it can be financially motivated, and response is typically the jurisdiction of law enforcement agencies. Within each of these categories, different motivations as well as overlapping intent and method of various actors can complicate response options. Criminal, terrorists, and spies rely heavily on cyber-based technologies to support organizational objectives.[163]

As the US and Europe have banded together, China and Russia have found each other to be necessary partners. Both have established strong and competent cyber forces. China understands that without

---

[162] *The Intercept*, 06 September 2016
[163] Cyberwarfare and Cyberterrorism: In Brief, Catherine A. Theohary, John W. Rollins, *Congressional Research Service*, March 27, 2015

cyber power, the influence of the United States in Asia and Europe cannot be held in check. China helped North Korea in developing cyber capabilities, and helped Pakistan in countering India's cyber-attacks on state-owned computers. In 2017 and 2016, in 19 Chinese universities, more than 20,000 Pakistanis received cyber terrorism training.

Every major nation is working feverishly to secure its national critical infrastructure, policing and intelligence data networks, but cyber-attacks from rival states and criminals continue. A research paper in 2012 described the formulation and function of Chinese cyber strategy:

> China's strategy of cyberspace warfare was formulated in the previous decade as part of a profound modernization process undertaken by the Chinese military. Based on the awareness that when it comes to kinetic warfare the Chinese armed forces are structurally inferior to the armed forces of the West, such as the United States military, the strategy reflects the understanding that in order to confront an enemy with technological superiority in the area of information flow, it is necessary to disrupt the enemy's access to this information. The approach involves dealing an opening blow comprising a cyber-attack, an electronic attack, and a kinetic attack on the enemy's information web and military technology centers. Such a blow will lead to the creation of blind spots on the enemy's part, allowing Chinese forces to operate with greater efficiency. The Chinese assumption is that by disrupting the flow of information it is possible to cause significant damage to the capabilities of a sophisticated enemy and gain an advantage in the early stages of a confrontation.[164]

International media reported the professional units of Chinese military establishment that support various operations in the cyberspace, and support a worldwide campaign of the army. The PLA General Staff Department's Third Department where thousands people work is the center of cyber operations across Asia. Chinese cyber strategy reflects the understanding that in order to counter the US army and its allies with modern technological superiority in the cyberspace, it is mandatory to undermine the access of US army and its information war experts to the PLA sensitive information. In the International Journal of Multimedia & Its Application, Robert Lai

---

[164] What Lies behind Chinese Cyber Warfare, Gabi Siboni and Y. R. *Military and Strategic Affairs Volume 4, No. 2*, September 2012

and Dr. Syed Shawon M. Rahman documented the threat of Chinese cyber terrorism, espionage and its worldwide hacking networks:

> China cyber-attack is an emerging threat to the national security of the US since the US has no dominance in cyber domain, while China goes on the offensive in cyberspace. The air, land and sea, and space domain are all interdependent on cyber infrastructure in order to be effective. A full spectrum cyber security strategy depends on an analytic of China cyber-attack by examining its dynamic strategic advantage and critical competitive advantage. . . Cyber espionage activities by Chinese hackers are on the rise, and it is widespread to all American, business, industry, and government sectors. Attack on supply-chain is not a task that non-nation-state hacker can easily achieve since it requires huge resources and technical skills.[165]

Cyberspace is both a physical and virtual domain. With the innovation of new hardware and software technology, cyberspace changes and evolves. At present, technological development forced several states to establish cyber armies to defend their national security and protect intelligence and industrial information.

During his China visit President Obama stated: "Our relationship has not been without disagreement and difficulty. But the notion that we must be adversaries is not predestined." This platitude is hard to reconcile with the fact that the US has by far the world's largest navy and is not shy to continue patrolling waters adjacent to China, tacitly threatening its vital international trade, while decrying any effort by China to develop systems of any kind that might be used in defensive or offensive operations of its own.

Chinese cyber intelligence has been targeting computers of several states to retrieve important financial and military information. The country's army has been investing billions dollar on its offensive cyber system, and trains hundreds of thousands experts to fight in the cyberspace effectively. Phil Muncaster in his InfoSecurity Magazine report noted:

> The PLA would likely use electronic warfare, cyberspace operations (CO), and deception to augment counter-space and other kinetic operations during a wartime scenario to deny an adversary's attainment and use of information. Chinese military writing describes informationized warfare as an asymmetric way to weaken an adversary's ability to acquire, transmit, process and

---

[165] *International Journal of Multimedia & Its Application* (Vol. 4, No. 3 June 2012). Robert Lai and Dr. Syed Shawon M. Rahman

use information during war and to force an adversary to capitulate before the onset of conflict.[166]

Mr. Gabi Siboni and Y. R elucidate Chinese cyber war for information gathering beyond its borders:

> The last six years have seen more than a few cyberspace attacks attributed to China, which apparently were intelligence gathering operations. An analysis of these attacks affords a means to identify China's basic attack techniques and infer its policy and methods. The attacks portray a world power intent not on focusing on a specific target, rather on gaining wide infrastructure access. In the case of Operation Aurora, the goal was to gain access to Google's password mechanism and the versions control software...The techniques identified in the well organized attacks were highly similar, using social engineering, exploiting software weaknesses, and inserting delay mechanisms to expand intra-organizational access and extract information. [167]

With the innovation of the Stuxnet virus in 2010, criminals and even merely mischievous members of the public and media attention were frequently drawn to tales of hacking and espionage. This virus has become a threat to national computers, and security and national critical infrastructure internationally. This virus was used in attack on Iranian nuclear sites. Over fifteen Iranian facilities were attacked and infiltrated by the Stuxnet worm. It is claimed that this attack was initiated by a random worker's USB drive. One of the affected industrial facilities was the Natanz nuclear facility.[168]

Britain, which is one of the guarantors of the territorial integrity of Ukraine after the Western-backed coup there, is being heavily criticized for its flawed approach to the expanding flare-ups along Europe's borders. In the Euro-committee of the House of Lords, the Cameron administration was deeply criticized for a 'catastrophic misreading' of the mood in Russia. As the recent growing political

---

[166] *Daily Times*, 23 March 2015

[167] What Lies behind Chinese Cyber Warfare, Gabi Siboni and Y. R. *Military and Strategic Affairs Volume 4, No. 2*, September 2012

[168] "Cyber Terrorism–Electronic Activism and the Potential Threat to the United Kingdom." A. Wareham and S.M. Furnell, "Advances in Communications, Computing, Networks and Security": Volume 5, Network Research Group, University of Plymouth, United Kingdom, and "Cyber Security and the UK's Critical National Infrastructure." A Chatham House Report, Paul Cornish, David Livingstone, Dave Clemente and Claire Yorke, September 2011. The Royal Institute of International Affairs, London. "Stuxnet Worm Attack on Iranian Nuclear Facilities," Michael Holloway, Stanford University, winter 2015.

tension in Ukraine changed the parameters of Russian and US priorities, the intelligence war has evolved. As a US ally, the UK is facing the challenge of Russian intelligence networks on its soil.

Interestingly, one of the most important functions performed by British intelligence is to provide timely warnings of hostile intelligence agencies present in the country. In the 1980s and 2000s, MI5 and MI6 were monitoring Russian intelligence networks in Britain. In fact, intelligence relations between the UK and Russia deteriorated since 2006, following the murder of former KGB agent Alexander Litvinenko in London.

In 2013, when the British Prime Minister visited Moscow, the intelligence agencies of both sides agreed to renew limited cooperation, but they did not proceed. The relationship turned hostile with the imposition of sanctions against Russia. Crimea rejected the West's imposition of a new regime in Ukraine. When Crimea voted to leave Ukraine and rejoin Russia in March 2014, Britain suspended all military cooperation with Russia.

The West continues to stoke the embers of the cold war, seemingly hoping to move to a hot war in spite of all. On January 24, 2015, the FBI charged three men with serving Russia in New York. These agents, the US newspapers reported, were directed to collect intelligence about the US sanctions against Russia.[169]

Some significant events in Europe and Asia recently occurred that left a deep impact on EU intelligence cooperation. In 2017, a new wave of attacks by "lone wolves" has raised concern, as this type of attack is nearly impossible to foresee or forestall. If an individual acts on his own, there is no communication with team members to be intercepted; and there is no money trail to follow. The threat in Europe now is the most extensive and dangerous the continent has ever seen, due to the massive influx of migrants allowed into the EU. However dire the plight of most migrants may be, and however much a socially-responsible citizenry may wish to help them, it cannot be denied that this massive migration has provided cover for elements who seek to harm our society. Their involvement in recent terror-related attacks in Brussels, London, Manchester, France, and Germany have raised serious questions, whether they truly act as disgruntled individuals or as agents controlled by certain interests. The majority of people who

---

[169] On January 24, 2015, the FBI charged three men with serving for Russia in New York. *Daily Times*, 07 January 2015

entered the EU and the UK used false documents and information to hide their identity. Britain learnt a lot from these consecutive EU intelligence failures and adopted an intelligence-led operational mechanism against terrorists and radicalized elements.

The emergence of a new culture of violence in tandem with a foreign-sponsored intelligence war means that the blame game and empty promises, accompanied by a useless blanket of intrusion in the name of "intelligence surveillance," are no help to anyone. To restore the confidence of citizens in the police force and community policing, the communities need to be involved in law enforcement process and well-thought through professional security measures are needed along with appropriate new technologies.[170]

We live in a land of multiple races, colors and cultures, but we have failed to mix the colors and forge a unified society. We still look at each other as aliens and have no interest in understanding each other's concerns; we do not purchase from each other's shops, and we do not exchange views and thoughts. This is the basic challenge that UK and EU citizens face today. We have failed to manage the increasing population burden, violence, and so many other law enforcement challenges that deeply affected our social stratification.

The ISIS bomb-making manuals are freely available online and its financing through the Internet has become a serious issue. The commissioner of the Metropolitan Police, London, Sir Bernard Hogan Howe, recently warned that the Internet is becoming a "dark and ungoverned" place for terrorists to safely operate. "Encryption on computers and mobile phones is frustrating police inquiries and leaving parts of the web as 'anarchic places'", Mr. Bernard said. In 2012, the UN reported noted: "The Internet may be used not only as a means to publish extremist rhetoric and videos, but also a way to develop relationships with, and solicit support from, those most responsive to targeted propaganda."[171]

Though our law enforcement and intelligence agencies are struggling to develop sophisticated tools to prevent detect and deter terrorists' online activities; the issue of mass surveillance in our society has become a headache. We are unable to walk unfettered as mass surveillance has tied our hands and feet, and confined us to a specific domain. From our e-mail box, Face book profile, Twitter

---

[170] *Telegraph* London, 17 December 2016
[171] *Daily Times*, 10 November 2014

feed and telephone to bedroom, nothing is safe. On 28 October, 2014, Chatham House, an international affairs think tank, organized an event on mass surveillance and counter-terrorism, in which UN Special Rapporteur on Counter-terrorism and Human Rights Dr Ben Emmerson and Chairman Intelligence and Security Committee of the British Parliament Sir Malcolm Rifkin were the main speakers.[172]

The debate started with the violation of privacy and massive surveillance blankets in the US, Europe and the UK. Dr. Ben Emmerson raised serious questions about the way UK and US surveillance mechanisms operate. The revelations of the new chief of the GCHQ, Robert Hannigan, in his Financial Times article, further complicated the issue when he categorically said that privacy has never been an absolute right. British Foreign Minister Philip Hammond also admitted in his statement before the Parliamentary Intelligence and Security Committee that the bulk data collection did not amount to mass surveillance.[173]

On 29 August, 2014, the UK Prime Minister warned that his country faced the "greatest and deepest" terror threat in history. Mr. David Cameron said that the risk posed by ISIS will last for "decades" and raised the prospect of an expanding terrorist nation "on the shores of the Mediterranean". Privacy and human rights groups complain that these day-to-day changing surveillance mechanisms might possibly alienate citizens from the state. On 01 September, 2014, Prime Minister David Cameron announced a series of new anti-terror measures. In fact, this announcement was the introduction of new powers to be added to the current terror laws.[174]

---

[172] On 28 October, 2014, Chatham House, an international affairs think tank report
[173] Ibid.
[174] On 01 September, 2014, Prime Minister David Cameron announced a series of new anti-terror measures. the *Guardian*, 01 September, 2014,

Chapter 7. A New Industry of Information Theft and the Prospect of Cyber Warfare in Britain and Europe

Cyber terrorism in the United Kingdom and EU caused fatalities, financial losses, and an unfolding threat to military industry. The UK and EU critical infrastructure and banking sectors have often came under attack from terrorists in and outside the border. Spies, criminals and foreign agents rely heavily on cyber-based technologies to support organizational objectives. They are state-sponsored terrorists engaged in cyber-attacks to pursue their objectives. Cyber spies are those who steal information and sell it in an open market. They target banking sector and industry. In 27 March 2015, the Congressional Research Service published a brief research paper on cyber terrorism, which highlights different aspect of cyber warfare:

> Cyber terrorism can be considered "the premeditated use of disruptive activities, or the threat thereof, against computers and/ or networks, with the intention to cause harm or further social, ideological, religious, political or similar objectives, or to intimidate any person in furtherance of such objectives.". . . Transnational terrorist organizations, insurgents, and jihadists have used the Internet as a tool for planning attacks, radicalization and recruitment, a method of propaganda distribution, and a means of communication, and for disruptive purposes. These individuals often work at the behest of, and take direction from, foreign government entities. Targets include government networks, cleared defense contractors, and private companies.[175]

---

[175] "Cyberwarfare and Cyberterrorism: In Brief." Catherine A. Theohary and John W. Rollins, Congressional Research Service, March 27, 2015

On 2 April 2017, Telegraph reported on the threat of cyber terrorism:

> Britain's airports and nuclear power stations were told to tighten their defenses against terrorist attacks in the face of increased threats to electronic security systems. Security services issued a series of alerts warning that terrorists may have developed ways of bypassing safety checks. Now there are concerns that terrorists will use the techniques to bypass screening devices at European and US airports. There were also fears that computer hackers were trying to bypass nuclear power station security measures. Government officials have warned that terrorists, foreign spies and "hacktivists" are looking to exploit "vulnerabilities" in the nuclear industry's Internet defenses.[176]

Information theft is a new industry that has developed worldwide, and it threatens the banking and financial sectors especially. As society has become dependent on IT technology, attacks on the state computers have intensified, causing financial damage in the UK and in Europe. From 2011 to 2017, cyber espionage caused the greatest transfer of wealth in history.

Britain is an easy target of cyber terrorism; various institutions recently reported the vulnerability of their computer data. In 2015, the country had a billion websites hosted by organization and individuals which generated new ideas, new threats, viruses and operations for their own purposes. These websites were considered a bigger threat to the institutional computers of numerous states. In 2013 and 2014, phishing, malware, and viruses attacked thousands of states owned computers and disrupted their networks.

The UK and EU governments are struggling to counter such attacks, but without the cooperation of private sector, they cannot target hackers and their networks. This irregular warfare in cyber space is challenging enough to national security operations. Private cyber-militias are in the field with professional skills that are able to use cyber-attacks on behalf of states in order to achieve their political goal.

Sometimes, when cyber terrorist attacks succeed it doesn't mean that state agencies failed; intelligence agencies always struggle to maintain the order and quickly respond to any terrorist attack. Now, if intelligence failed then we need to reform it and reorganized its function.

---

[176] 2 April 2017, *Telegraph Report*

The threat is evolving and emerging in modern forms. From e-mail to confidential documents protection, every possible threat to the computers of organizations and businesses need proper consideration. Cyber-attacks cannot be prevented as the hackers operate from a safe distance and have various ways to mask their identity and their location. The cost of fighting such attacks is enormous. But the cost of identity theft and other breaches is even greater. The level of US data breaches hit a record high of 783 in 2014.[177]

During the last two decades, cyber attacks affected one hundred private and government institutions websites in the United Kingdom and EU and caused millions of pounds in damage. Now the issue is even more important, since every government collects massive amounts of data on their citizens, firms, political and financial organizations, health and social sectors, organizations and groups of all sorts, ethnic communities and rival institutions. This data can be used well — for national security, tax collection, demographics and international geopolitical strategic analysis — or for malign purposes.

Quizzical public statements of the British government about the vulnerability and insecurity of the country's population and critical infrastructure support the conventional belief that the country is under constant threat. Every month, newspapers publish lurid statements about the extremist culture across the country, and officials continually demand more funds to fight it. We have some 85 terrorist networks and 34,000 radicalized elements operating across the country, but counter-terrorism authorities and police say they know little about all these terror nests.

To combat financial cyber-crime, Britain's Cyber Security Strategy was published in November 2011, which underlined the technicality of the threat faced by the country's institutions from economic jihadists and state-sponsored cyber forces. The basic objectives of the UK Cyber Security Strategy are to introduce the traditions of partnership and transparency both across business and within the international community in an effort to meet the growing cyber threat. Security Service (MI5) recently warned that cyber-crime, espionage and cyber terrorism pose a major threat to the national security of the country.

We have been told that intelligence agencies play an important part in helping to tackle the threat of economic warfare, but numerous complaints from various state institutions, including defense and

[177] Identify Theft Resource Centre Report

foreign ministries, indicate that the campaign against information warfare has been less effective in the past. Reports tell us that we are constantly at risk of cyber espionage from China, India and North Korea.

State and private institutions have been experiencing cyber-attacks against their websites for a decade, and new groups of financial hackers are training new techies to wage war against the global financial markets. These are skilled, educated experts in cyber warfare, and have the capability to destroy and disrupt any financial network around the world by hacking into the servers of state institutions and private companies and using those servers, unbeknownst to the provider or proxy servers.

Experts see cyber-crime as an unauthorized network that breaches data. In 24 November 2014, cyber-attack on Sony Entertainment and on sensitive computers in the UK and US illustrate the difficulties in categorizing attacks and formulating a response policy.[178] Cyber warriors disabled all information technology system of the Sony Entertainment. In the UK cyber security strategy ("Cyber Security Strategy Protecting and Promoting the UK in a Digital World-2011), government specified four objectives: to "tackle" cyber-crime, to be "more resilient" to cyber-attacks, to maintain a "stable and vibrant" cyberspace, and to achieve cross-cutting knowledge, skills and capability to underpin all its cyber security objectives.[179] But the government has been unable to professionally fight cyber terrorism since the commencement of its cyber security strategy.

Former GCHQ director Professor Sir David Omand suggested:

> Maintaining community confidence in the action of the state is important. Good pre-emptive intelligence can reassure the community by removing the extremists and by disrupting any potential attack without having to fall back on the sort of blunt discriminatory measures that alienate moderate support within the community on which effective policing and counter terrorism depends.[180]

Government and law enforcement agencies are increasingly concerned about the possible cyber-attack from extremist groups, foreign hackers and intelligence networks with malicious intent,

---

[178] *New York Times*, 17 December 2014
[179] The Cyber Security Strategy, Protecting and Promoting the UK in a digital world-2011
[180] *Securing the State*, David Omand, 2015

such as terrorism and act of disruption. Chief of GCHQ once warned about the cyber threat to the UK security and said the country's economic security is under threat. Mr. Lobban warned that the country is witnessing the development of criminal market place, where cyber dollars are traded in exchange for citizen's credit cards details. In present global marketplace, Internet is no longer just about e-mail and website. This machine empowers the growing list of revenue-generating e-business activities. In the near future, cyber terrorism and economic warfare will ultimately target all Britain state institutions.

The Internet is emerging as a security threat to all nations as terrorists can easily communicate through Internet and receive instructions. The Internet is widely regarded as a center of information, a bigger library, asset of literature, but it can also serve as a resource for dangerous information. In these circumstances, both the US and UK have introduced strict surveillance measures to tackle the threats emanating from the Internet or online activities. Chancellor George Osborne recently suggested that MI5 and MI6 must concentrate on cyber terrorism and devote more money and manpower defending Britain from the cyber-attacks of hostile states.

In a London Conference on Cyberspace, experts agreed on the point that the threat to information security in the UK and Europe has intensified. Former British Foreign Secretary William Hague issued a laughably weak warning to countries involved in financial terrorism, saying this undeclared war was "unacceptable." Likewise, Prime Minister David Cameron politely called on such opponents to just "please stop it." No wonder the public is not convinced their security is in good hands.

The threat of cyber terrorism has generated panic around the globe. The financial markets, banking sectors, and national critical infrastructure are under threat from cyber attackers representing various nationalities. Over the last decades, several technologies have been developed that pose serious threat to states and private institutions.

In 2011, Chatham House, a UK think tank, published a detailed report on the evolving threat of cyber terrorism to the country critical national infrastructure. Its researchers asked different question in their survey to find out how this menace needed to be tackled and highlighted the legal aspects and possible counter measures. The United Kingdom National Security Strategy (NNS), and Strategic Defense and Security review (SDSR) released in October 2010 promoted cyber security to a Tier One risk to national security, and its high status was reinforced by the UK government's allocation of £650 million to cyber security and intelligence. The UK Ministry of Defense's December 2010 Green Paper entitled "Equipment, Support and Technology for UK Defense and Security noted that perhaps the over-riding characteristics of cyberspace are the space of change.[181]

Drumming up fears over another hypothetical risk, on 02 April 2016, Prime Minister David Cameron warned that ISIS may possibly be planning to use drones to spray nuclear materials over Western cities. The Telegraph reported that there was growing concern among world leaders that extremists are looking to buy commercial drones to launch a dirty bomb attack over major metropolitan cities. US officials reportedly fear that extremists could steal radioactive material from a medical facility and sell it through the "dark web." Prime Minister Cameron said Britain would deploy counter-terrorism police and the UK Border Force while British leaders held a Cobra meeting. Mr. Cameron said at the summit that Britain planned to hire 1,000 more armed police and deploy counter-terrorism units in cities outside London to help counter any possible attack.[182]

The UK Defense Secretary wowed that his country would spend £40 million on a new cyber security center designed to protect Ministry of Defense networks and systems from "malicious actors." "Britain is a world leader in cyber security but with growing threats this new operations centre will ensure that our armed forces continue to operate securely," Fallon said. The UK think tank Privacy International (PI) called on the government to use targeted surveillance to tackle threats from terrorists and organized criminals rather than collecting people's private online data. The UK and United States will take part in a joint exercise.

---

[181] Cyber security and the UK's critical national infrastructure, Paul Cornish, David Livingston, Dave Clemente, and Clair Yorke, a Chatham House Report, September 2011, and also, The role of the national security council in developing the national security strategy and strategic defense and security review, 21 October 2010, Chatham House Report London. https://www.chathamhouse.org/events/view/156871#sthash.2ttMyWPN.dpuf
[182] *Telegraph* 01 April 2016

The attacks in Brussels raised fresh concerns about the prospect of nuclear terrorism, with fears Islamic State militants may attempt to get hold of materials to create a 'dirty bomb'. But the cyber-attack exercise with the US would ensure that both governments and their civil nuclear industries were prepared and could address any potential weaknesses. The Prime Minister said terrorists would "like to kill as many people as they possibly could" amid fears Islamic State jihadists could attempt to create a dirty bomb.

The lack of an international agreement among states on cyber terrorism is thwarting efforts to bring hackers to justice, according to the UNODC report. The report's focus is cyber warfare; cyber groups and young hackers those use the Internet for terrorist purposes. They distribute propaganda to incite violence: "Governments need to work together to stop cyber-attacks and operating systems must be redesigned," Eugen Kaspersky, the founder of Kaspersky Lab warned. Kaspersky, whose lab discovered the flame virus that has attacked computers in Iran, told reporters in Tel Aviv University: "It's not cyber war, it's cyber terrorism and I'm afraid it's just the beginning of the game...I'm afraid it will be the end of the world as we know it."[183]

Under this program, GCHQ, MI5, NSA and FBI would try to improve information sharing, cooperate with each other and fight cyber terrorism with competency. However, there were speculations that the Islamic State could carry out cyber-attacks. Daily Mail reported George Osborne as saying that: "ISIS could kill British citizens by launching cyber-attacks on hospitals and air traffic control." Osborne said that if ISIS attacked, it would disrupt all government systems including, hospitals, and satellite and air traffic control."[184]

On 14 July 2014, Britain allocated £1.1 billion for defense to fight cyber terrorism. David Cameron ordered the armed forces to fight the unseen enemy. "Britain military must be enhanced to defeat against the threat of terrorist attacks as well as the potential for extra immigration if 'fragile and lawless state fracture,' Mr. Cameron warned. There are cyber networks operating in the country with the ability to acquire invisible quantities of sensitive data of various state institutions. These networks might be linked to some states.

---

[183] Daily Times, 10 December 2012
[184] ISIS plot to use cyber jihadists to bring down airlines and target UK nuclear power stations and hospitals, Daily Mail, 17 November 2015

These countries have trained thousands of cyber warriors for cyber-attacks on the institutional networks of other states and establish strong economic espionage networks. The US and UK have failed to meet these challenges. In the UK, the GCHQ changed its strategy by establishing an academic research institute in partnership with research councils global uncertainties programme (RCUK) and the department of business innovation and skills. This newly established institute to counter the cyber aggression of China in Britain is still in the process of improvement. Whitehall is unsure what to do and how to respond. Intelligence agencies demand a £ 2. 1 billion budget for 2014–15. In 2014, government announced a £ 650 million strategy to protect the country from cyber terrorism, because the GCHQ reported that cyber-attacks targeting sensitive data in government institutions reached disturbing level.

Chancellor George Osborne suggested that MI5 and MI6 need to concentrate on cyber terrorism and devote more money and manpower to defending Britain from the cyber-attacks of hostile powers. However, the case is different here as the intelligence and security committee in 2015 warned that much of the task to secure the country's networks in cyberspace was still at an early stage. The Foreign Secretary warned that organized attacks on a daily basis against government networks were more irksome. On 06 September 2012, he launched a government guide to cyber security for business. The UK has developed weapons to counter the threat from hackers, William Hague said.[185]

On 17 November 2015, George Osborne decided to double the budget to finance fight against cyber terrorism while refusing to confirm that budget cut to be announced soon. The United King had to spend £1.9 billion over five year countering ISIS and its use of Internet to plan attacks against the government installations. In his GCHQ office speech, Mr. Osborne said GCHQ offensive capabilities to counter ISIS would be improved. The GCHQ was told to work with the Defense Ministry to develop countering techniques against the ISIS use of Internet.

But British intelligence agencies have limited manpower. Only 12,700 people are not sufficient force to fight the ISIS, but they are

---

[185] The UK has developed weapons to counter the threat from hackers and will strike first to protect itself, *The Inquirer*, 18 October 2011 http://www.theinquirer.net/inquirer/news/2118012/uk-strike-cyber-warfare-foreign-secretary

competent. On 23 November 2015, Prime Minister David Cameron presented Britain's National Security Strategy and Strategic Defense and Security Review (SDSR) in Parliament, and said that the world is more vulnerable than the last five years. The United Kingdom has been experiencing cyber-attack on it state computers since a decade. Cyber warriors continue to attack private sectors as well.[186]

---

[186] On 23 November 2015, Prime Minister David Cameron presented Britain's National Security Strategy and Strategic Defense and Security Review (SDSR) in Parliament, and said that the world is more vulnerable than the last five years.

CHAPTER 8. THE EU MODE OF OPERATION: INTELLIGENCE SURVEILLANCE MECHANISMS, NATIONAL SECURITY CRISIS AND THE CONSEQUENCES OF BREXIT VOTE

The EU is a most complex and competitive project, a unique conglomeration of independent and sovereign states. As rewarding as its successes have been the alliance suffered a crisis in terms of mutual security and integration after the Brexit vote.

Intelligence as an element of the EU's security governance is subject to the dynamics of networks which emerged in a specific institutional context in response to the objectives shared by the project partners. Globalization and technological progress prompted free movement in a borderless world on the continent but also generated opportunities for terrorist and extremist elements.

The globalization and digitalization during the last decade resulted in an increasingly interconnected and interdependent world. More and more information seekers are gaining access to technology and data, and all these technological and political networks have become a major cause of far reaching social and political transformation in the region. The geographical expansion of the Islamic State in South Asia, notably in Afghanistan and parts of Pakistan, and the participation of EU nationals in its wide-ranging operations prompted a changing security dynamism, geographical crisis, and spread of violence and separatism.

The Taliban's shifting loyalties have also changed the mechanical motion of the new cold war and put in danger the enlargement of the Pakistan–China Economic Corridor through Central Asia and

Afghanistan. Pakistan and China face numerous internal security challenges, including extremism and ethno-nationalist violence, and they do not have full control over Taliban and Uyghur Islamic Movement in Chinese Central Asia. The arrival of immigrants in EU cities from these war zones, and their attacks on public places, raised important question about the changing intelligence and counter-terrorism measures in member states.

Citizens criticize the huge budget allocated to the operations of intelligence agencies and police forces across Europe, and the failure of Europol to demonstrate in a professional manner in order to interdict these attacks. The credibility of the EU as a comprehensive crisis manager needs some legal changes in term of its ability to put forward timely and effective action to respond to crisis and threats. In other words, the key to security is effective states that provide for the security of their citizens, if they do not, tension will arise and internal conflicts will emerge.[187]

The EU faces an increasingly an insecure and instable neighborhood. The war in Syria, Iraq and Afghanistan, humanitarian crisis in the region and the weakening of state structure have created many problems like the invasion of refugees and infiltration of extremist and terrorist forces into the region. The EU may further face deteriorating security environment and an unprecedented level of threat, while the Brexit has made the security of the project complex. Germany and France face a wide range of security challenges including the lone-wolves attacks and radicalization, which prompted wide-ranging legal and administrative reforms in these two states. In December 2016, Germany, France and Italy proposed a multilateral cooperation in the field of intelligence sharing to counter extremism and radicalization in Europe. The EU member states collectively established three competent institutions to make effective the process of intelligence sharing.

Intelligence cooperation among the EU member states has always been underwhelming due to different stakeholders bureaucratic policies and personal interests. On EU level, the issue of intelligence sharing is very complicated as every state showed reservation about their national secrets protection while sharing with the member states intelligence and law enforcement agencies. Researcher Bajorn

---

[187] *Daily Times*, 10 January 2017

Fagersten (2015) in his paper documented important point about the EU intelligence system:

> Scholars of institutional design suggest that when some states contribute more to an institution than others... They will demand more sway over the institution. Other states will grant this control to ensure their participation. Such hierarchical control can reduce the autonomy loss for powerful states and mitigate the risk of free riding and other collective action problems by allowing some states to monitor others. Elements of hierarchy may thus offer net intelligence gain for an organization such as the EU, as long as it empowers actors with high-quality intelligence capabilities. To a large extent, this was the case in the building of IntCen.[188]

In some member states, bureaucratic circles also have interests that need to be served otherwise they create bigger challenges and intercept the process of intelligence cooperation on law enforcement level. Their resentment towards some member states, and personal interests prompted further strain in relations among member states. The EU intelligence also embroiled in multifaceted crisis as every member state agencies revolves around its own government interests and do not want to share national secret with another state. These stakeholders are private policing and intelligence partners who influenced institutional policies, and control some aspects of international cooperation. Regardless of their political and religious affiliation, there are bureaucratic elements in some states who want to facilitate cooperation among states. They sense that intelligence cooperation among EU states is an important weapon against extremism, terrorism and suicide attacks. Having analyzed the performance and importance of European intelligence Centre (INTCEN), John M. Nomikos writes:

> European Union Intelligence Centre (INTCEN) joined the European External Action Service (EEAS) in 2010, but it has a far longer history. Its origin, as "a structure working exclusively on open source intelligence (OSINT)", lie in the Western European Union (WEU), an intergovernmental military alliance that officially disbanded in June 2011 after its function were gradually transferred over the last decade to the European Union's Common Security and Defense Policy (CSDP). In 2012 INTCEN's predecessor organization

---

[188] *The Guardian*, 05 July 2016

was established as a directorate of the General Secretariat of the EU Council and given the name EU Join Situation Centre (SITCEN). [189]

The immediate reaction to the April 2017 terrorist attack in Paris, and in May and June 2017 in London and Manchester consecutively called for a structural intelligence reforms, and intelligence cooperation on law enforcement level in Europe. French politicians warned that the country faced war like situation. The current migrant crisis, lack of reforms and lack of intelligence-led policing caused more challenges. The recent Paris, Brussels, London, and Istanbul attacks and extensive intelligence war in Britain also raised important questions as to the credibility and unprofessional demonstration of intelligence and counter-terrorism agencies across Europe. Britain's internal security threats have become more acute, notwithstanding the burgeoning multifaceted surveillance system, intelligence-led policing, TEMPORA, MENWITH HILL and private security system in partnership with local policing authorities. Terror-related incidents have not gone away. The presence of mightiest infrastructure MENWITH HILL on Britain soil with a staff of more than 2,200 personnel — the majority of which are Americans — did not help us in overcoming the evolving national security challenges. [190]

The Snowden revelation regarding mass surveillance in the European Union generated an unending debate while media in 2013 began publishing his documents. His revelations exposed several states spying on their own citizens. The NSA and GCHQ came under severe criticism by mainstream society across EU and the US. There has been an intense debate in European electronic and print media about the underwhelming Achilles heel operational mechanism and tactics of their intelligence agencies. The involvement of EU agencies in power abuse, over-activation, politics, and corruption has made their performance absurd.

After the terrorist attacks in Paris, French intelligence changed it legal framework. Before these attacks, French intelligence was operating without a comprehensive and coherent legal framework to streamline its operational mechanism. Keeping in view the intelligence

---

[189] "Intelligence and decision making within the Common Foreign and Security Policy," Bjorn Fagersten, European Policy Analysis, Swedish Institute for European Policy Studies, October 2015
[190] European Union Intelligence Analysis Centre (INTCEN): Next Stop to an Agency? John M. Nomikos, http://rieas.gr/images/editorial/NomikosEUintelligence15.pdf.

needs, on 24 July 2015, French government promulgated a new law and incorporated with the existing law. France has six intelligence agencies, in which three receive directions from defense Ministry, and two agencies receive directions from Finance Ministry, and one is under the Ministry of Interior. Interception communication in France is large scale due to the exponentially growing trend in extremism and radicalization. In Germany, the case of intelligence gathering and interception communication is quite different from France. In Germany, intelligence agencies have no police powers.

In Germany, there are three intelligence agencies two of which focus on domestic intelligence, and one on foreign intelligence. German intelligence was unable to intercept terrorists entering the country. Intelligence agencies came under serious criticism in 2016, when extremist groups started killing innocent civilians in towns and cities. Netherlands maintain professional intelligence infrastructure that demonstrate under the guidance of policy makers and legal provisions. The country's intelligence has been regulated by the intelligence and security services act 2002. In 2016, this act came under scrutiny in order to streamline operational mechanism. The general intelligence and security services (AIVD) is under Ministry of interior, responsible for investigating individuals and groups that pose threat to national security, and gathering intelligence information. In AIVD's website, details of its operational mechanism and intelligence gathering technique are available.[191]

Netherlands has also adopted that strategy through a Comprehensive Action Program. The UK police counter-terrorism head, Richard Walton recently warned that the Berlin attacker cruised across Europe, which highlighted the vulnerability of the Schengen zone that allows terrorists to cross borders without restrictions. However, German intelligence recently confirmed the ISIS network in EU but experts understand that the attack was an intelligence failure. In 2016, Europe suffered multifaceted security crisis, including record arrival of immigrants from Asia, Africa and Middle East, and the Brexit, but the crisis of intelligence cooperation will continue in 2017 as there will be three elections in the coming months.

---

[191] Foreign Intelligence Gathering Laws: France, *Library of Congress Research Report*, https://www.loc.gov/law/help/foreign-intelligence-gathering/france.php

In April 2017, a radicalized supporter of Islamic State rammed a truck into a store in Stockholm killed four people and 15 injured. The police arrested a 39-year-old man of Uzbekistan heritage for complicity in the attack. After this attack, civil society criticized the police and law enforcement agencies for their failure to understand the trends of extremism and radicalization in the country.[192] There are more extremist cells in the country where young Swedish men are being recruited and prepared to challenge the authority of law enforcement agencies. The threat of terrorism and radicalization has intensified as thousands of radicalized cell shifted from Asia and Africa into the continent to wage jihad against the local population. In these circumstances, the EU intelligence has been in deep crisis since the UK and France attacks in April 2017. Terrorist groups are dancing in the streets of Europe and recruit young people in their cells. The issue of terrorism and mistrust among the EU member states, the flow of refugees to the region, and the trend of radicalization has put the security of the region in danger.

Following the London, Paris and Brussels, Manchester and London terrorist attacks, the EU member states demanded global response and proposed a security union to counter radicalization and extremism in all member states. France, Germany and some Eastern European states were very serious on this issue and demanded immediate action. Not only due to these attacks, is the EU facing more serious challenges of security cooperation and intelligence sharing, France and Germany reconsidered their stance on domestic security, and introduced security sector reforms to reinvest the professional intelligence and policing mechanism for combating domestic extremism. Notwithstanding all these security measures in Germany, France and London, the EU still faces obstacles to establish a unified security network, because all states have different priorities, resources and level of expertise when it comes to fighting lone wolves and extremism.

Over the last two years, terrorist incidents in EU increased due to mistrust among the member states. Intelligence cooperation on law

---

[192] In April 2017, a radicalized supporter of Islamic State rammed a truck into a store in Stockholm; he killed four people and injured 15. The Royal United Services Institute for Strategic Studies Report on Intelligence Failures spotlighted important aspects of French intelligence. "Paris: an Intelligence Failure or a Failure to Understand the Limits of Intelligence?" Timothy Holman, Commentary, 14 December 2015.

enforcement level has been one of the most problematic areas of the EU counter radicalization efforts, but there are signs of improvement on sharing security information as some states have taken this issue seriously. As Europol is unable to propose a professional panacea to the exponentially growing danger of lone wolves attacks, member states are reluctant to share their national secrets with it. There are other reasons including the defense of sovereignty in matters of national security that is buttressed by a culture of secrecy and the independence of national services, which expressed concern that secret information and method of work could be compromised if intelligence is widely shared.

On 30 March 2017, Guardian reported British Prime Minister warning to the EU leaders that failure to reach comprehensive Brexit agreement will result in a weakening of cooperation on crime and security. In response to her remarks, Brussels criticized and said the British government had no right to blackmail Europe. "If, however, we leave the European Union without an agreement, the default position is that we would have to trade on World Trade Organization terms. In security terms, a failure to reach agreement would mean our cooperation in the fight against crime and terrorism would be weakened", Theresa May said.[193]

Policy experts and intelligence analysts across Europe have recognized the motives of lone actors, and proposed wide-ranging security measures to counter the emerging threat. The EU border existence is now in crisis after terrorist attacks in Germany. France is facing waves of Middle East-bound terrorism, and Germany has border problems with Poland. Spain is in deep water. The country has not been exempted from the lone-wolves attacks. The UK is one of the first country that enacted administrative measures in the context of counter-terrorism, but terrorists and lone wolves still dancing in the streets.[194]

There are thousands immigrants who live in EU and Britain with fake identities-involved in criminal activities. The Tunisian terrorist

---

[193] On 30 March 2017, *The Guardian* reported British Prime Minister warning to the EU leaders that failure to reach a comprehensive Brexit agreement will result in a weakening of cooperation on crime and security. Brussels criticized her remarks and said the British government had no right to blackmail Europe. "London Attack a Reminder of Fear for Post-Brexit Security Cooperation," *Reuters* 23 March 2017

[194] On 30 March 2017, *The Guardian* reported British Prime Minister warning to the EU leaders

Amri who killed innocent civilians in Germany had 14 identities. Terrorists will attack Britain and some EU member states in 2017, because Brexit played a key role in destabilizing the project, but the country will also face a multifaceted crisis. Terrorist forces have intensified their efforts to select targets in Britain, because they have a good number of supporters inside the country. Chemical and biological attacks cannot be ruled out as explosives experts have entered Europe and are trying to cross the border into Britain. Recent report of Europol warned that France remains high in the target list of ISIS aggression, but fatalities will be inflicted on Germany, Netherlands and Britain in near future.

CHAPTER 9. RISKS RELATED TO RADICALIZED ISIL FIGHTERS WHO
RETURN TO THE UK AND EUROPE

The return of radicalized fighters from Syria and Iraq is certainly not new, recent civil war in Persian Gulf and Middle East regions have put radicalization and jihadism back on the European Union's security agenda. The crisis is now a greater challenge of the security and integrity of the EU. Jihadism and returnees are generally perceived as an Islamic radicalization that supported Islamic State (ISIL) and Al-Nusra. In 2016, radicalized groups in Balkans started joining the ISIL without any legal restrictions and limitations. This elucidates the question of and treatment of foreign fighters by Western Balkan governments. When these groups developed capabilities of using biological and chemical weapons, they returned to the EU to operate in a violent mode. Researchers by Jelena Beslin and Marija Ignjatijevic highlight the development of radicalization in Europe:

> The seeds of radical Islam were planted with the formation of the
> *El Mujahid* battalion within the Bosnian Army, comprised of extremist
> foreign fighters. After the war, charitable organizations funding
> mosques and educational establishments, based in or backed by Gulf
> States, started flourishing across the Balkans. The commencement
> of the dissemination of conservative Salafi interpretation of Islam,
> which resulted in a substantial outflow of foreign fighters to militant
> Islamist groups in Syria and Iraq. Moreover, years of war fuelled
> by nationalistic rhetoric, and the proliferation of organized crime
> networks amidst the ruined economy of the region, had turned some
> fighters into 'dogs of war'. Despite the fact that former fighters from
> the Balkans occasionally fought on foreign battlefields, they were

usually regarded as volunteers or 'seasoned soldiers' and did not face any penalties or wider societal condemnation. Only with the emergence of Balkan jihadists fighting for Daesh did the question of foreign fighters come under the spotlight in the region.[195]

The establishment of different sectarian, extremist and radicalized networks in Europe such as ISIL, Al Nusra, Al Shabab, Boko Haram, Lashkar-e-Toiba, Sipah Muhammad, Sepah Sahaba and Taliban, have put the security and stability of the whole region at risk. Now, these groups are openly dancing in the streets of EU member states with impunity, and threaten all those who write against their terrorist operations. Recently, in Manchester, London, Brussels and Germany, these elements killed hundreds of innocent civilians, and created the climate of fear. European intelligence agencies have been unable to control the affiliation of their young citizens with the Islamic State (ISIL). These trained fighters openly challenge the authority of law enforcement. Jelena Beslin and Marija Ignjatijevic spotlight some states of Eastern Europe where ethnic and sectarian groups making things worse:

> Although Western Balkan countries were affected by these phenomena in different ways, the contingents of foreign fighters reflected the region's fragmented ethnic and religious structures. Countries with large percentages of Muslims — Kosovo, Bosnia and Herzegovina, and Albania — are ranked among the top five European 'exporters' of foreign fighters to the Middle Eastern battlefields when measured against their population size. In total, estimates show that around 1,000 individuals originating from the Western Balkans have ended up among the ranks of different militant groups in Syria and Iraq, mostly Daesh and Al-Nusra Front. When it comes to the war in Ukraine, the numbers are lower, however in comparison to Syria and Iraq, the conflict has attracted significantly fewer foreign fighters in general. . . .Balkan jihadists are mostly young people, typically between 20 and 35 years of age, coming from remote rural areas, usually poor and unemployed, with little work experience or skills to offer. Being marginalized and stigmatized in deeply divided societies burdened with the legacy of war also accentuates the vulnerability of these individuals to Islamist propaganda.[196]

---

[195] Brief Issue: Balkan foreign fighters: from Syria to Ukraine, Jelena Beslin and MarijaIgnjatijevic, European Union Institute for Security Studies (EUISS) June 2017
[196] Ibid.

Balkan nations have amended their criminal laws and outlined comprehensive counter-terrorism strategies. Kosovo, Bosnia and other nations proposed tenacious punishment for the jihadist returnees from Iraq and Syria, and reviewed counter terrorism mechanism. The above mentioned groups collect money from shopkeepers, businesses firms, their members, and those individuals who support their atrocities in the Persian Gulf. The outflow of foreign fighters to these conflict zones reached its peak between 2013 and 2015, after which the numbers dropped sharply. Researcher Fabien Merz describes motives behind the jihadist inclination towards Islamic State: "Since the start of the civil war in Syria and the resurgence of the conflict in Iraq, around 30,000 "foreign fighters" have joined jihadist militias fighting in these conflicts. Around 5,000 of them are from European countries. Many have joined IS, which has, amongst others, the stated goal of carrying out attacks in the West... Thus, today more than ever, the question arises of how to deal with a potential increase of jihadist returnees and the concomitant security and societal challenges".[197]

The availability of chemical and biological weapons to terrorist and radicalized organizations in Europe has become a matter of serious concern for policy makers, as the ISIL used these weapons in Iraq and Syria in 2016. On many instances, Lone wolves tried to obtain biological weapons but failed. The ISIL in 2016 claimed responsibility for the attacks at Brussels' Zaventem Airport and Maelbeek metro station: "A number of soldiers from the Caliphate — carrying explosive belts, bombs and automatic weapons, and targeting locations chose with precision in the Belgium capital, Brussels — entered Zaventem Airport of Brussels and a subway station in order to kill a high number of crusaders. They then detonated their explosive vests in the middle of a crowd. The outcome of the attacks was 40 dead people and no less than 210 injured people". A former US army captain, Ms. Carole House in her recent paper (2016) explained the illegal trade of biological and chemical material in some Eastern European states:

> Nonetheless, vulnerabilities in legitimate states' control of radioactive material may present opportunities for IS. As IS exploits its territorial holds over areas with civil infrastructure and gains more recruits abroad, it might be able to steal cesium-137, used in cancer therapies, from hospitals. Law enforcement has intercepted

---

[197] Analysis of Security Policy, Fabien Merz. 210, June 2017, Centre for Security Studies (CSS), ETH Zurich

attempts by criminal organizations to sell cesium-137, believed taken from Russian hospitals, to IS. Illicit trade offers IS potential access to materials not currently within their reach. There are concerns in Iraq and some Western countries over reportedly stolen iridium-192, and Belgian authorities have speculated that IS operatives are searching for places in Europe to steal radioisotopes to use in an RDD. IS's control over territory provides it access to industrial areas with toxic industrial chemicals and laboratory facilities that could enable the development of biological toxins or chemical agents. Dual-use chemicals such as chlorine are relatively easy to acquire and can be disseminated via aerosols and other crude, easily developed methods. IS's geographical location in Syria and Iraq, countries that likely hold undisclosed stockpiles of old chemical munitions, also could facilitate IS's acquisition of complete chemical munitions that it could deliver via artillery systems.[198]

As the threat of jihadism in Europe intensified, and the ISIL started training more young jihadists, this act of the terrorist organization created the climate of fear. As we have witnessed terror incidents but recent attacks in Europe and the United Kingdom raised important questions that if the ISIL and local extremist groups retrieved biological and chemical weapons, it will inflict huge fatalities on civilian population. Final report of the Taskforce on Combating Terrorist and Foreign Fighters Travel of the Homeland Security Committee (September 2015) describes details of terrorist attacks, return of foreign fighters to the United States, Australia and Europe with new zeal and ideologies:

> Foreign fighters have contributed to an alarming rise in global terrorism by expanding extremist networks, inciting individuals back home to conduct attacks, or by returning to carry out acts of terror themselves. For instance, one prominent British foreign fighter killed this year in Syria was linked to terrorist plots spanning the globe, from the United Kingdom to Australia, without ever having left the Middle East. In another case, an American from Ohio was arrested in April after returning from Syria to plan an attack on a U.S. military base, where he intended to behead soldiers. This case is part of a broader challenge. Indeed, since early 2014 more than a dozen terrorist plots against Western targets have involved so-called "returnees" from terrorist safe havens like Syria and Libya. Foreign fighters are also the motive power behind the growth of ISIS. Despite a year of U.S. and allied airstrikes, the group has held most of its

---

[198] "The Chemical, Biological, Radiological, and Nuclear Terrorism Threat from the Islamic State." Carole N. House, *Military Review*, September-October 2016

territory and continues to replenish its ranks with outside recruits. . . The level of terrorist travel we are seeing today, however, is without precedent. The numbers are now so high that Western governments are becoming increasingly worried they will be unable to prevent violent extremists from entering their countries undetected. Federal Bureau of Investigation (FBI) Director James Comey warned last year that we need to brace ourselves for a wider "terrorist Diasporas" out of Syria and Iraq.[199]

In 2015, more than 100 jihadists were sent to prison in France. French Interior Ministry said these jihadists wanted to constitute attacks in the country. 421 radicalized jihadists were incarcerated. The threat of lone wolves is quite a new trend developed by the ISIL leadership in Europe. Terrorism changed dramatically in recent years. Attacks by groups with defined chains of command have become rarer, as the prevalence of terrorist networks, autonomous cells, and, in rare cases, individuals, has grown. In his CSS analysis (June 2017), Mr. Fabien Merz describes the de-radicalization efforts of Denmark:

> Despite considerable efforts in the area of prevention, Denmark is one of the European countries most severely affected by the phenomenon of foreign fighters (around 143 individuals have left the country since 2012, which per capita, puts Denmark in second place behind Belgium in Europe). Aarhus, the country's second city, was especially affected, with 31 jihadist volunteers leaving by 2013. Subsequently, a new model was developed based on the structures and cooperation networks that have existed in Aarhus for decades between the police, educators, and other actors in the sphere of violence prevention. On the one hand, it aims at preventing young people from joining groups like IS. On the other hand, an integrative approach is also adopted in order to de-radicalize and reintegrate jihadists into society after their return. Since 2014, this program has been open for returned jihadist fighters on a voluntary basis, provided they have not committed any crimes and have been screened and assessed as not posing any security risk. Participants can be supported in finding a job as well as housing and can also be provided free psychological and medical care. Specially trained mentors (including former jihadists) play an important role as reference persons for the returnees and support them in not only dealing with everyday life, but can also offer religious counseling.[200]

---

[199] Final Report of the Taskforce on Combating Terrorist and Foreign Travel, Homeland Security Committee, September 2015
[200] The CSS Analyses in Security Policy No. 210, June 2017, Centre for Security Studies (CSS), ETH Zurich

In May 2017, Switzerland law enforcement authorities were aware of the jihadist returnees to the country from Syria and Iraq. These returnees caused misunderstanding between the Muslim and Christians communities. The ISIL leaders have justified the killing of non-Muslims in Europe. However, in October 2014, Switzerland outlined some legal strategies, amended laws and adapted new legislations to effectively counter jihadist terrorism. Some of these measures, including the obligation to report to the police on a regular basis, were also applied in connection with jihadist returnees. In October 2015, the second report of TETRA emphasized on the draft of a comprehensive strategy against radicalized forces in the country. However criminal proceeding in the Switzerland against the acts of terrorism and radicalization are under the jurisdiction of Federal Administration.

The Balkan states law enforcement administration is weak and divided between Islam and Christianity, which caused jihadism and radicalization. In all five states, more than 500 fighters travelled to Iraq and Syria for fight against the national armies of the region. This region is a fertile ground for Islamic State and Al Nusra terrorist groups. According to the Balkan Investigative Reporting Network (BIRN), more than 900 radicalized elements from all five countries participated in a so called jihad in Iraq and Syria. Researcher and Executive Director of the Belgrade Centre for Security Policy, Predrag Petrovic spotlighted elements from Balkan participated in Syrian war:

> Balkan countries are among Europe's top exporters of volunteers fighting for radical Islamic organizations such as Daesh and Jabhat al-Nusra. The Balkan Investigative Reporting Network (BIRN) estimates that over 300 fighters from Kosovo have travelled to warzones in Iraq and Syria, while 330 fighters have come from Bosnia and Herzegovina, 110 from Albania, 100 from the Former Yugoslav Republic of Macedonia, and 50 from Serbia and 13 from Montenegro. This places Kosovo and Bosnia and Herzegovina as the top two European countries by percentage of population who has joined terrorist organizations, while Albania is ranked in fourth place just behind Belgium.[201]

There are so many programs of countering radicalization in Europe that differ greatly from one another in terms of aims, structure. These programs have so for been ineffective in countering radicalization

---

[201] Islamic radicalism in the Balkans. PredragPetrovic, 2016, European Union Institute for Security Studies (EUISS) June 2016.

and extremism. Nevertheless, their experience to date, points to certain key characteristics and challenges. The recent London and Manchester attacks showed how the UK counter-terrorism strategy failed to address radicalization in the country; the same experiment can be found in other EU member states, where terrorist and extremist forces often challenge the authority of law enforcement agencies. The involvement of Saudi Arabia in Europe and its support to extremist and terrorist organizations raised several questions including the distribution of millions dollar Saudi fund to the mosques of European states. On 28 November 2016 One Europe reported:

> Bosnia and Kosovo are two of the biggest Islamist exporters in the Balkans who are joining ISIS and al-Nusra Front (al-Qaeda's affiliate in Syria). In the case of Bosnia, when the war broke out in the early 1990's an Islamist movement was Saudi-sponsored with foreign mujahedeen fighters who were mobilized to fight along the Muslim Bosnians against both the Serbs and Croats. Some of these foreign fighters received citizenship and stayed in Bosnia after the war which created a root of Islamists in the country. . . Kosovo's story of extremist Islamic infiltration is similar to Bosnia's. During the 1998–1999 Kosovo war, foreign mujahedeen fighters took part in the war alongside the Albanian Kosovar Muslims against the Serbs, although in lesser numbers than in Bosnia. As the conflict came to an end, a handful of Saudi -faith based funds were circulating in Kosovo. The money was used for providing humanitarian aid: hospitals, schools, orphanages but also to build Wahhabi mosques. Saudi Joint Relief Committee for Kosovo and Chechnya (SJRC) whose activities have been linked to al-Qaeda, "reportedly built ninety-eight primary and secondary schools in rural Kosovo in the first few years after the war." The Kosovo government believes at least 300 Kosovars have fought with Islamist groups in Syria and Iraq.[202]

In all EU member states, different counter-terrorism strategies have been adopted. Governments outlined mechanism and designed legal measure to fight against the violent ideology of foreign fighter returning from Iraq and Syria. These measure and strategies are of great importance, but the basic weapon that can effectively counter these radicalized elements is intelligence sharing, which the EU member state did not fully exchange information. International Centre for Counter-terrorism (ICCT), in its Research Paper-April 2016 discussed the phenomenon of foreign fighters returning from Syria and Iraq:

[202] One Europe, 28 November 2016

Threat Perceptions in the EU and the Member States According to various official EU documents, four general aspects of the FF phenomenon were identified to pose a threat: 1) Persons travelling from the EU to Syria/Iraq seeking to become a FF; 2) the threat posed to EU countries by returned FF who had acquired basic military training and battle field experience; 3) the impact of the FF phenomenon and related terrorist activity on social cohesion within the EU; and 4) the threat posed by would-be FF, who, having been prevented from travelling to Syria/Iraq, may carry out attacks within the EU instead. The majority of MS consider the FF phenomenon as a serious security risk to their national society. Fourteen MS make use of threat-level assessment mechanisms. Only five regard the threat level in their country to be low or below average. Eleven MS have changed their threat levels since 2011, when the Syrian conflict commenced and the issue of FF started to increasingly gain attention.[203]

On 17 November 2016, the Independent newspaper reported London and Portsmouth among Europe's most notorious hubs for terrorist recruitment. A new study by the US based combating Terrorism Centre (CTC) spotlighted the existence of ISIL sympathizers in several places where immigrant communities live. Analysis of more than 850 foreign fighters showed that almost three-quarters came from cities where at least one other militant was known, often as part of the same friendship group. Out of the jihadists known to have travelled to Syria and Iraq between 2011 and 2015, the highest number came from London; the newspaper quoted CTC report. Terrorist killed and incarcerated in Britain were Ifthekar Jaman, Assad Uzzaman, Mehdi Hassan, Hamidur Rahman and Mamunur Roshid and Mashudur Choudhury–Jaman. The skills and abilities of these radicalized people to train fighter are based on the deprivation of Muslim communities. "The ability of jihadi groups to recruit foreign fighters is thus based on creating a narrative that is focused on the ongoing deprivation of Muslims, both in specific Western polities, as well as in the international arena," the report warned.[204]

However, having responded to the threat of foreign terrorist fighters, Council of the European Union outlined comprehensive

---

[203] The Foreign Fighters Phenomenon in the European Union Profiles, Threats & Policies, International Centre for Counter-terrorism, The Hague (ICCT), Research Paper April 2016
[204] *Independent*, 17 November 2016

strategy in 2015. After the Paris terrorist attacks, leaders of the EU held a debate to design a joint mechanism. On 25 April 2017, the Council adopted a directive on control of the acquisition and possession of weapons. On 9 June 2017, the Council adopted conclusions on improving information exchange and ensuring interoperability of EU information systems. The mechanism focused on three areas of action:

1. Ensuring the security of Citizens
2. Preventing radicalization and safeguarding values and
3. Cooperating with International partners-1, Council of the European Union: Response to foreign terrorist fighters and recent terrorist attacks in Europe.

When the ISIL intensified its efforts of recruiting you Muslims from all EU member state, in August 2014, the European Council concluded that Islamic State was a direct threat to the security of the European countries. Travelling to Iraq and Syria for fight against local population was believed to contribute to the radicalization of a person and to his or her acquisition of capabilities to carry out a terrorist attack, as well as also potentially being a factor in the prolongation of the conflict.[205]

The involvement of Qatar and Saudi Arabia in the internal affairs of the EU member states, and their funding of terrorist organizations prompted misunderstanding between Islam and Christianity. Saudi Arabia has been financing Takfiri groups in Eastern and Western European states since 1990s. After the fall of the Soviet Union, Pakistan, Turkey, Saudi Arabia reached Kosovo, Bosnia and Serbia to support Muslim groups against the Christens. Pakistan played important role by providing arms and ammunition to the Bosnian Muslim fighter against Serbs by air, mostly from Jalalabad airport in 1990s. In his Telegraph news analysis, David Blair describes the Saudi and Qatar financial support to some terrorist and extremist organizations in Europe:

> General Jonathan Shaw, who retired as Assistant Chief of the Defense Staff in 2012, told The Telegraph that Qatar and Saudi Arabia were primarily responsible for the rise of the extremist Islam that inspires ISIL terrorists. The two Gulf states have spent billions of dollars on promoting a militant and proselytizing interpretation of their faith derived from Abdul Wahhab, an eighteenth century

---

[205] Council of the European Union: Response to foreign terrorist fighters and recent terrorist attacks in Europe

scholar, and based on the Salaf, or the original followers of the Prophet. But the rulers of both countries are now more threatened by their creation than Britain or America, argued Gen Shaw. The Islamic State of Iraq and the Levant (ISIL) has vowed to topple the Qatari and Saudi regimes, viewing both as corrupt outposts of decadence and sin. So Qatar and Saudi Arabia have every reason to lead an ideological struggle against ISIL, said Gen Shaw. On its own, he added, the West's military offensive against the terrorist movement was likely to prove "futile". "This is a time bomb that, under the guise of education, Wahhabi Salafism is igniting under the world really. And it is funded by Saudi and Qatari money and that must stop," said Gen Shaw.[206]

On 18 January 2016, Daily Express reported former British Prime Minister admitted that Saudi Arabia funded schools in Britain. Cameron said, "We need to look very carefully... it is already illegal for anyone to fund extremist groups in our country. We ban, proscribe, extremist groups.... I think if you look at what Saudi Arabia is doing, they have a good programme for de-radicalizing people who have become radicalized and terrorists".[207]

US President Donald Trump warned that the survival of the West is at risk as he lashed out at hostile forces ranging from Islamic terrorism to Russia, statism and secularism during a speech in Poland. Grandstanding at the start of a high-stakes, four-day trip to Europe, the US president gave a highly nationalist address in Warsaw, warning that a lack of collective resolve could doom an alliance that endured through the Cold War. "As the Polish experience reminds us, the defense of the west ultimately rests not only on means but also on the will of its people to prevail," Trump said at the site of the 1944 uprising against the Nazis. "The fundamental question of our time is whether the west has the will to survive."

According to the political risk analysis firm, SEERECON report, Saudi Arabia distributed more than $800 million among various personalities and organization in Bosnia: "Meanwhile radical imams began to provide something akin to life coaching, and in some towns, dormitories opened to provide accommodation to poor students and spread Salafist and Takfirist ideas. In the eyes of certain segments of the impoverished populations of the Balkans, the representatives

---

[206] *Telegraph*, By David Blair, 04 Oct 2014
[207] *Daily Express*, 18 January 2016

of these Islamic organizations began to have more credibility than government institutions".[208]

In German foreign policy website, information about radicalization and extremis is available in detail. On 07 June 2017, the website highlighted the salafist jihadist elements and their operational capabilities, and spotlighted their fund raising campaign:

> In Kosovo, according to a report appearing in the US press last year, Saudi-orientated clerics began spreading Salafist Islamic teachings soon after the NATO invasion in 1999. They had "a lot of money" and a lot of Salafi literature, and built a lot of mosques. 240, of the over 800 mosques, have been built since the war, with long-standing moderate imams being replaced by Salafis, oriented on the Saudi model of Islam. As usual, also in Kosovo, the Salafist crusade has reinforced jihadism. From 2014 to the spring of 2016, alone, 314 Kosovars have been identified, who have gone abroad to join the Islamic State, the highest number per capita in Europe. Officials ascribe this radicalization clearly too Saudi influence.[209]

Recent terrorist attacks in Belgium are the sign of the existence of jihadist organization in the country. More than 380 Belgians travelled to Syria as foreign fighters. Security situation in the EU and the United Kingdom has deteriorated. Every day we read stories of terror acts across Europe, but never heard about the joint strategy and sincere intelligence sharing of member states against terrorism. The evolving and revolving national security approach of the British government has put the lives of citizen in danger. The lacks professional security sector reforms. Intelligence agencies of the country operating on various directions to find a solution to the prevailing violent culture in the country, but the way they tackle society does not help them in maintaining law and order. Bulgaria Analytica in 2016 published an article of analyst Alex Alexiev that highlights the establishment of Wahabi sect in Balkans, and the financial support of Saudi Arabia to various radicalized and jihadist organizations:

> In fact, it is not possible to comprehend the serious inroads made by terrorist organizations in the Western Balkans, as expressed in the hundreds of jihadists from the region in Syria and Iraq, without reference to the preceding radicalization of Muslim communities

---

[208] The Islamist zero-hour: The unique threat posed by Isis has been analyzed in depth. But how should the West respond in practice? John Jenkins, *New statesman*, 2 September 2015
[209] German foreign policy website, 07 June 2017

under Saudi auspices. The original Saudi involvement in Bosnia stems from its heavy funding of a Sudanese 'charity' called the Third World Relief Agency (TWRA) led by El Faith Husanein, a man known to be a friend of Bosnian president Izetbegovic and a financier of Al Qaeda. According to Western sources, between 1992 and 1995, TWRA is reported to have supplied $2.5 billion worth of weapons and supplies to Bosnia. Direct Saudi involvement in Bosnia begins in 1993 with the founding of the Saudi High Commission for Relief of Bosnia and Herzegovina under the leadership of the current king of Saudi Arabia, Prince Salman bin Abdul Aziz al Saud. Similar Saudi front organizations were installed also in Albania and Kosovo. The High Commission under Prince Salman engaged in the spreading of the radical Wahhabi creed in Bosnia to the tune of $600 million, of which $120m came from the private account of Salman. During this time, the commission was implicated in close ties with Al-Qaeda in terms of both funding and recruitment of jihadists.[210]

In May 2017, Salman Abedi attacked an Ariana Grande concert at the Manchester Arena killing at least 22 people. Investigators believed the 22-year-old Briton, who had Libyan ancestry, acted independently but may have been assisted by ISIS. There are 30,000 jihadist terrorists mostly born in Britain, pose serious threat to the national security of the country. There is a wide body of literature stemming from different disciplinary backgrounds that explores where children get their religion, values or culture and what family characteristics strengthen their transmission. Pakistani jihadist organizations are using Britain as an arena of fund raising and developing influence. Lashkar-e-Toiba, Hezbul Mujahedeen, Sapah Sahaba, Sepah Muhammad, Taliban, and other organizations receive millions dollar fund from the UK based business firms and traders. Members of these organizations go to Kashmir, Syria, Iraq and Afghanistan, and kill innocent men, women and children there. In 2013 after the Woolwich terrorist attack, the term 'Londonistan' re-entered the political discourse of the country.

Radicalization of Muslim population in the EU member states raised important question including the inattention of successive governments in countering the exponentially growing terrorist networks of jihadists and lone wolves. Recent studies seeking to understand it suggest of the need to profile the processes of recruitment, be it online or in places such as schools, mosques and prisons. The causes of radicalization in Europe, and the process of

---

[210] Saudi Funding of Radical Islam, Alex Alexiev, *Bulgaria Analytica*, July 29th, 2016

recruitment by jihadist organization are not new; the EU radicalized organizations have been recruiting their member in Afghanistan, Kashmir, Syria and Iraq since 1990s. The process of recruitment occurs by way of extremist propaganda spread by terrorist groups with roots abroad, but operating in Europe. This is serious issue but the EU member states including Britain have never tried to counter thus hydra through a professional security approach.

Today, the EU is center of radicalization, extremism, jihadism, and nuclear black market, and finds itself on the frontline in the fight against this hydra. The EU has not yet succeeded in establishing an intelligence agency and collective counter terrorism mechanism due to their mutual distrust. In London, Manchester, France, Germany and Belgium, as well as in Turkey, Tunisia, terrorists carried out attacks and killed hundreds of innocent civilians, but European leadership never took the issue seriously. These attacks spotlighted the exponentially growing culture of radicalization within the EU Member States that challenged the authority of the police. The danger emanating from jihadists has now become one of the most precarious security threats in the continent. A growing number of former foreign fighters, jihadists, as well as their handlers and facilitators and those who aspired to join them, are being tried and sentenced to prison terms in the region. In Manchester and London, terrorists targeted innocent civilians– and like other jihadist attacks in Europe it exposed, once again, the major challenges faced by security services. They are challenging the writ of the government and even the writ of the state.

Information technology and globalization generated opportunities for the terrorists to further develop their operational capabilities and to cooperate in some cases for the implementation of illegal aims. The story of countering terrorism and radicalization with a traditional mechanism looks quite complicated in several EU member states as European intelligence agencies never shared all national secrets on terrorism with each other wholeheartedly. If the EU member states follow the US mechanism of countering terrorism or deal with the hydra individually, they can face numerous difficulties because the US war on terror strategy have already failed and caused misunderstanding between the Muslim world and the west. However, relations between the EU with the United States on the intelligence cooperation level cannot produce more successful strategy against the common threats which put in risk European and international security and peace.

European states suffered from a number of weaknesses. These include a lack of expertise in languages such as Arabic and a lack of engagement with Islamic communities which hinders the ability to develop human-intelligence sources. Terrorist attacks in London and Paris once again contradicted the free movement of terrorists the EU and the lack of EU-wide intelligence sharing. Due to their earlier criminal activities, most perpetrators of the attacks in both London and Paris were known to intelligence in the EU member states. The EU is in crisis due to the Brexit and its complications. Britain is muzzy to leave the EU or not, but one thing is clear the country want to return to the project by a proper way. In his European View article (03 May 2016), researcher Oldrich Bures highlights hindrances in sharing intelligence among EU member states:

> Intelligence sharing has arguably been one of the most problematic areas of the EU's counter-terrorism efforts. While there appear to have been gradual improvements over time, Europol has certainly struggled to transcend the traditional obstacles to intelligence sharing, and national security and law enforcement agencies are still too often reluctant to share 'high-grade', real-time intelligence on terrorism that can be acted on immediately. This is primarily due to the persistence of nationality in international policing and intelligence. Although numerous Council decisions and Commission proposals include an obligation for EU member states to share information, in practical terms, this duty has had little impact because it cannot force member states' authorities to share more information, that is, intelligence that has not previously been disseminated. This is also confirmed by Europol officials: 'We know that [national] intelligence services cannot share personal-related and operational-related data with us because of their very strict data protection regimes and there is no use talking it over' (interview with a Europol official, September 2009).[211]

As elucidated earlier, the threat of nuclear and biological terrorism in Europe existed. In these pages I want to highlight the threat of Jihadists returning from Syria and Iraq with new thoughts and ideologies. Now, the threat of dirty bomb in the EU is making headlines in newspapers. The availability of dirty bomb material in an

---

[211] Researcher Oldrich Bures, European View, 03 May 2016

open market in some Eastern European states, and in one investigation in Chisinau, Moldova, samples of uranium-235 and cesium-135 were seized by police. On 06 April 2017, The Time Magazine published an investigative report on the possibility of dirty bomb attacks in Europe. The report focused on the smuggling of dirty bomb material in Eastern European states:

> The danger from dirty bombs is spreading even faster. For starters, they pose none of the technical challenges of splitting an atom. Chaduneli's type of uranium was particularly hard to come by, but many hospitals and other industries use highly radioactive materials for medical imaging and other purposes. If these toxic substances are packed around conventional explosives, a device no bigger than a suitcase could contaminate several city blocks—and potentially much more if the wind helps the fallout to spread. The force of the initial blast would be only as deadly as that of a regular bomb, but those nearby could be stricken with radiation poisoning if they rushed to help the injured or breathed in tainted dust. Entire neighborhoods, airports or subway stations might need to be sealed off for months after such an attack. Obama's successor is certainly alive to the nuclear threat. In a Republican primary debate in December 2015, Donald Trump said the risk of "some maniac" getting a nuclear weapon is "the single biggest problem" the country faces. But he suggested that the world would be safer if more countries acquired nukes.[212]

Recent reports confirmed the availability of enriched uranium and dirty bomb material in some Eastern European black markets, which is causing anxiety and fear. The ISIS and Taliban are struggling to purchase or retrieved these materials through their networks, and use it against government and public installations. After the London, Manchester (2017) and Brussels attack in 2016, there were reports that ISIS was seeking radioactive materials to inflict more fatalities on civilians. However, for ISIS, developing a dirty bomb from radioactive material is not a difficult task. The Associated Press reported that Eastern European gangs are exploiting the strained relations between Russia and the United States to sell radioactive materials to ISIS. On 04 March 2016, France24 reported terrorists seeking material of dirty bomb.

A strong sense of fear and disappointment has filled the air in Europe's streets, markets and towns. The ISIL fighters kill innocent

---

[212] On 06 April 2017, *Time Magazine* published an investigative report on the possibility of dirty bomb attacks in Europe

civilians with impunity. They are so called Islamists who kill men, women, and children in the name of God. The death toll is mounting as a result of escalated spate of suicide attacks across the continent. People are affected mentally or physically. The ISIL fighters ushered in stoking violence, which was not common in Europe, through targeting different groups of communities on the grounds of their creed. Too many tears are flown and too much blood is shed as terrorists pursue their sinister aims at the cost of countless of civilians' life.

The so called Islamists intensified their attacks without showing any sign of mercy to non-combatants, mainly women and children. It is an undeniable fact that children have nothing to do with war or religious faith. But they are killed in cold blood perhaps on the basis of their race or caste. Life has no value for terrorist groups. In other words, the radical ideology of militant fighters feeds on violence and blood. The ISIL jihadists want large-scale terror attacks and focusing primarily on European targets. Attacks in the EU, both by lone actors and terrorist groups, are possible. Estimates of intelligence agencies indicate several dozen people directed by IS may be currently present in Europe with a capability to commit terrorist attacks.[213]

With the establishment of thousands of mosques in Europe, the networks of jihadist terrorist organizations expanded. They received huge funds from these mosques and spent them to purchase weapons for their fighters, and sent to their terrorist networks in Pakistan, Somalia, Sudan, Nigeria, Kashmir and Syria. Analyst Giulio Meotti (2017) in his Gatestone Institute paper has proposed professional counter terrorism measures, elimination of unnecessary mosques, religious schools, deporting radical imams, and draining the welfare financing of EU jihadists, banning foreign funding of mosques and religious schools, and closing some religious and political nongovernmental organizations across Europe:

> Radical Islam is the greatest threat to Europe since Nazism and Soviet Communism. But we still have not been inclined to question any of the political or ideological pillars that have led to the current disaster, such as multiculturalism and mass immigration. Hard counter-

---

[213] What really lies behind the surge in Isis-inspired attacks across Europe: Security and intelligence agencies are struggling to cope with a lethal new threat, Independent, Kim Sengupta, 27 July 2016. http://www.independent. co.uk/news/world/europe/isis-terror-attacks-uk-security-ansbach-munich-nice-germany-a7158886.html, Isis has dozens of fighters in EU, security experts warn, London Evening Standard, Martin Bentham, 02 December 2016, and *Daily Outlook*, 17 June 2017.

terrorism measures, the only ones that could break the terrorists' plans and morale, have never been taken. These would include shutting down mosques, deporting radical imams, banning foreign funding of mosques, closing toxic non-governmental organizations, draining the welfare financing of Europe's jihadists, refraining from flirting with jihadists, and stopping foreign fighters from returning home from the battlefront. We treat war and genocide as if they are simply mistakes made by our intelligence agencies. We dismiss radical Islam as the "mental illness" of a few disturbed people. Meanwhile, every week, two new Salafist mosques are opened in France, while radical Islam is preached in more than 2,300 French mosques. Thousands of European Muslims have gone off to wage jihad in Syria and Iraq, and fundamentalists are taking control of mosques and Islamic centers. In Brussels, all the mosques are controlled by the Salafists, who are disseminating radical Islam to the Muslim masses.[214]

The EU may further face deteriorating security environment and an unprecedented level of threat, while the Brexit has made the security of the project complex. Germany and France face wide range of security challenges including the lone wolves attacks and radicalization, which prompted wide-ranging legal and administrative reforms in these two states. As the terrorists continue to mount threats to physical security, the response is also expected to remain focused on employing greater force. This is also making it more challenging for EU power elites to take on the terrorists in their ideological and intellectual spaces. The Islamic State is making such a shift as matter of necessity, as consolidating and expanding the core state may no longer be an option. European research reports indicated that terrorists, mostly of European origin, were instructed by the ISIL leadership to construct "interlocking terror cells," select target, and mechanism. Now, these lone wolves and groups in all EU member states try to take the tactics of insurgency to the streets of Europe.

Since January 2015, jihadist terrorism killed 239 people in France. Perspective on Terrorism (2016) noted the return of 1,750 jihadists from Middle East. There are reports that more than 5,000 European fanatics travelled to Syria and Iraq with between 15 to 20 per cent dying on the battlefield. Up to 35 percent returned. Between 2014 and 2016, radicalized jihadists killed 273 people, and between 2015 and 2016, jihadists carried out 14 attacks. Moreover, the Paris and Brussels

---

[214] Europe Fights Back with Candles and Teddy Bears, Giulio Meotti, 28 May 2017, https://www.gatestoneinstitute.org/10430/terrorism-candles-teddy-bears

attacks in November 2015 and March 2016 were probably the first case since 1995 of the same jihadist cell being able to strike hard twice.

Some reports revealed that since the establishment of the ISIL in Iraq and Syria, more than 27,000 foreign fighters believed to have travelled to Syria and Iraq to take up arms alongside extremist groups such as the Islamic State, around 5,000-6,000 are estimated to be European. The EU's anti-terrorism coordinator, Gilles de Kerchove, once revealed that between 2,000 and 2,500 European jihadists are still operating in Syria and Iraq. On 19 September 2016 telegraph reported Rob Wainwright, director of the European Union's police agency Europol, told the Wall Street Journal that Western Europe will face the return of thousands of foreign fighters. He said their exposure to extreme violence "on top of their radicalized state makes them highly dangerous individuals". Intelligence agencies in the UK are preparing plans for the return of hundreds of UK nationals who went to fight for the ISIL.

Today there are more British Muslims in the ranks of ISIS than in the British Armed Forces. During 2015–2016, the ISIL-inspired lone wolves launched a series of terrorist attacks against European cities and killed more than 132 people and injured 352. For most of its history, the ISIL focused on Afghanistan, Iraq and Syria. It did call for attacks in the West in 2014. In early 2016, however, an ISIS spokesman declared that "the smallest action you do in the heart of the West is dearer to us than the largest action by us and more effective and more damaging."

The media, and consequently public attention, is largely focused on violent Islamist extremists; while this may reflect the broader threat, it is at odds with that from lone-actor terrorism. An important tool in combating the lone-actor terrorist threat is therefore ensuring the public is able to recognize his behavior and to report this behavior to the law enforcement agencies. The threat of lone wolf terrorists is a growing phenomenon and it represents a significant threat to EU member states. Following the attacks in Manchester and London, British intelligence expert Michael Whine said thousands of potential terrorists are on European checklists but Italian police are well aware of the threat. Intelligence agencies in the UK have prepared a watch list of more than 30,000 people, 3,000 of which are regarded as being potential terrorists.

CHAPTER 10. THE ORGANIZATION OF EU INTELLIGENCE

Most of the current intelligence problems within the European Union, whether they relate to predicting surprise attacks, the politicization of intelligence cooperation, or questions of ethics and privacy, are old conundrums. In fact, European intelligence infrastructures never tried to sincerely cooperate and share intelligence on national security, and never responded with Damascus-blade to the growing threat of radicalization in the region. However, closer attention to obvious lessons from the past would have assisted the intelligence apparatuses of these states in avoiding the Taliban, ISIS and other ethnic and sectarian groups and lone wolf attacks on civilian and military installations. After the London, Madrid, Paris, Munich and Nice attacks, the EU member states were waiting for miracles to bring a ready-made panacea to the pain of their citizens. The most critical counter terrorism efforts within the EU still need to be streamlined where law enforcement agencies have failed to share information properly.

The lack of security sector reforms, bureaucratic control of intelligence operations, government and private stakeholders, and ethnic and sectarian factors are the most important aspects of any intelligence infrastructure in a state, where these conflicting developments paralyze an intelligence agency. A clear distinction and division of tasks and responsibilities was needed between the external security policies and internal legislative and political measures and tools, an intelligible policy was also needed with regard to security, and a full parliamentary control over the operation and performance of intelligence agencies was has been a constant demand by civil society and intellectual forums.

The case of EU law enforcement agencies is not so different from the fact that in some Eastern European states old bureaucratic and ideological infrastructure is in place. With the development and growth of digital communication and cyber technology in Britain and Europe, they face serious threats from insiders within the government and private institutions as many terrorist and extremist groups have taken to cyberspace to train their young educated members in order to make access to sensitive government data.

They also pose serious threat to the missile and nuclear installations. They have developed professional capabilities to disrupt private, and state owned defense industries, police and operational nuclear communication, and create an uncontrollable security crisis. Thousands Asian, African, and Arabs have claimed asylum on fake documents, or became citizens of the UK and the EU, while police and other law enforcement agencies don't know about the actual background of these people. Were they terrorists, extremists, criminals, hackers, professionals, military officers, intelligence officers, cyber terrorism experts, police officers, intelligence operators, government officials, convicted terrorists/criminals, members of terrorist/extremist organization and nuclear scientists, the question of their actual background needs a detailed answer. The involvement of South Asian intelligence agencies in EU social and political issue, their lobbies in parliaments and social forums, and their leak of sensitive information is matter of great concern. These agencies support Asia candidates during election days, and then use them as a tool to influence the process of policy making in EU member states.

As Internet continues to play important role in our daily life and makes our life vulnerable, majority people in Britain do not know about the actual role of Internet in the country's political, military and social institutions. Britain and EU are under serious threat from insiders (foreign intelligence agents, spies, radicalized elements, extremists and parliamentarian) who know the secrets of state machine, and know about the political and social cycle of EU society. We understand the professional approach of the European Union and the UK to cyber terrorism, intelligence operation, and also understand their legal and political preparedness, but more legal and inter-governmental cooperation is needed to secure the important data of defense industry, missile and nuclear installations. British intelligence agencies and the police that foiled more than 15 terror-related plots during the last four years are struggling to professionalize their approach in combating the threat of cyber terrorism within the UK and Europe.[215]

The Paris terrorist attacks caused deep torment across Europe while intelligence agencies of all member states developed new counter terrorism measures to involve communities in decision making process. But insider threats remain a threat. Insiders who work in various state and private institutions in all European states have access to sensitive data and intelligence information; pose greater threat to the security of the state. They also pose serious threat to national critical infrastructure. British National Security Strategy for 2016-2021 has already warned that insiders are greater threat to the national security of the state:

> Of equal concern are those insiders or employees who accidentally cause cyber harm through inadvertent clicking on a phishing email, plugging an infected USB into a computer, or ignoring security procedures and downloading unsafe content from the Internet. Whilst they have no intention of deliberately harming the organization, their privileged access to systems and data mean their action can cause just as much damage as malicious insider.[216]

The Europol and Eurojust have also failed to deliver properly. The EU intelligence agencies complain that the Europol policing organization is unable to deliver, particularly in the field of investigation. Moreover, Europol has also failed to demonstrate itself as a professional policing organization after the Paris, and Germany attacks. One of the most important tasks of an intelligence agency is to investigate and provide immediate warning of foreign and domestic terrorist attacks while security of a country is at threat.

One reason for these failures is that intelligence and law enforcement agencies operate in opposite directions in a complex legal environment. There is huge difference between these agencies' perceptions of the "war against terrorism" in Iraq, Syria and Afghanistan. Europol and Eurojust are confused and don't know how to operate in collaboration with all the EU intelligence agencies. But

---

[215] *The Guardian* 06 March 2017
[216] British National Security Strategy for 2016-2021

the question is why the issue of political and bureaucratic stakeholders is not properly addressed?

Terrorists have repeatedly been able to carry out their attacks before being identified or, if marked as individuals of concern, intercepted, raising doubts about the effectiveness of counter-terrorism in Brussels, throughout Germany and the UK, and in France. There are so many hindrances, stakeholders, and political lords, due to which the EU member states cannot move ahead with a single voice. The Speculations that the security assurance of all member states within the EU is mere a hyperbole as complaints of some Easter European allies about the Brussels attitude raised several questions. The Netherlands, Denmark, Moldova and Baltic states feel threatened. There recent complaints against the weak intelligence sharing mechanism are matter of great concern. The Nice and Munich attacks further exposed the EU counter-terrorism approach, where political parties and civil society pointed to the incompetency of law enforcement agencies.[217]

Professional intelligence and law enforcement approach is not something ready-made and available in markets; it is built by experts and policy makers. The issue of security sector reforms in France and Germany is often discussed in print and electronic media, but in reality, their zeal and resolve are revolving around old mechanism. More than 24 years ago, some intelligence reforms were introduced in France under the 1991 law, while intelligence surveillance was confined to the tapping of wireless telephone communications. After that initiative, in 2015, an intelligence act was adopted by the French government, but after the terror attacks in 2015 and 2016, the country's parliamentary investigation identified multiple failures of French intelligence.

On 21 January 2015, French Prime Minister Manuel Valls presented a package of immediate reforms to address the issue of radicalization and terrorism in his country, but unfortunately, the new counter-terrorism measures did not prove effective to save the country. The recent security measures against Muslim communities had weakened

---

[217] On 21 January 2015, French Prime Minister Manuel Valls presented a package of immediate reforms to address the issue of radicalization and terrorism in his country, *the Guardian.*

the roots of French intelligence agencies and the lack of trust from the populace further added to the difficulty.[218]

In these new intelligence efforts, the government created the code of internal security within the intelligence act, which means to create the climate of trust between intelligence agencies and minority communities. The act stresses technical capabilities of the intelligence infrastructure to harmonies the range of tools that intelligence can use according to the regime applicable to judicial investigations. The failure of French intelligence before the 14 July 2016 terrorist attacks in Nice was mainly due to the lack of its coordination with law enforcement agencies to prevent the truck runner.

However, when the killings started, police and security agencies were unable to show a brisk reaction or intercept the truck immediately. All these attacks were carried out under the nose of police and intelligence surveillance system, which means something, is going wrong under the carpet. Chief of the French domestic intelligence warned in June 2016 that terrorist attacks are inevitable. In these circumstances, French law makers had no option other than to call for a shake-up of intelligence infrastructure of the country.

A committee of lawmakers in a press conference regretted on the lack of coordination between foreign and domestic intelligence agencies. "Our intelligence services failed," said a French lawmaker.[219] German intelligence is not so different from the French spy agencies. Their consecutive failures to intercept religiously or nationalistically motivated Muslim extremists before they translate their resentment into violent action thoroughly frightens the people and the government. In Moldova and Georgia, a security crisis and political fragmentation stand in the way of further EU integration. Foreign intelligence agencies have established secret networks in these two states and continue to influence policy making.

Moldova's support for EU integration is weak, while Georgia also sees that its citizens still face an uneven visa regime within EU member states. And, amidst this controversial engagement, German intelligence spied on France, and British intelligence spied on Germany, so that intelligence cooperation among EU states became a serious joke. On 06 November, 2013, BBC reported the head of German parliament's intelligence committee called for enquiries into

---

[218] BBC News 06 November 2013
[219] The Guardian 05 July 2016

alleged spying committed by the British embassy in Berlin. German intelligence agencies were looking at the US and UK through a hostile lens after the taping of Angela Merkel's personal telephone by NSA and UK's illegal surveillance operation in the country.

Britain's decision to leave the EU could have a significant impact on the Union's ability to help nations on its eastern borders, and implement political and economic reform. After the Paris, Brussels and Berlin terrorist attacks, the EU member states realized to establish a strong unified intelligence and security network, but things are not alike that we sensed as there were different priorities, resources and level of expertise within every state. Intelligence sharing among 28 member states is not an easy task as it seems, policy makers and secret services face numerous legal, technical and political obstacles. However, limited cooperation on security issues among all 28 states is a reminder that even after six decades of integration; the EU remains an implausible project. Intelligence cooperation and adverse relationship between the EU and UK will not cease after the Brexit as the UK contributes a lot in the field of intelligence and law enforcement.[220]

The UK has been a leading protagonist in shaping the nature of security cooperation under the auspices of the EU, as reflected in EU agencies and policy area. Chief of EU foreign policy struggled to start initiatives and setting up defense related research to reorganize the EU defense cooperation after Brexit. The UK decision to leave the EU provides an opportunity to use the provisions of the EU's Lisbon Treaty to move forward on one hand, and the UK exit from the project will be a serious loss of capabilities for the EU, making closer cooperation among member states, on the other.

On 17 January 2017, Prime Minister Theresa May's speech enraged the entire European Union. She was critical of the EU attitude towards Britain. "The UK cannot possibly remain within the EU single market as staying in it would mean "not leaving the EU at all", Theresa May said.[221] Her London speech and her subsequent visit to World Economic Forum in Davos raised several important questions including the UK intelligence and security cooperation with the EU.

---

[220] *Daily Times*, 07 February 2017
[221] *Telegraph*, 23 December 2016, On 17 January 2017, Prime Minister Teresa May's speech enraged the entire European Union. She was critical of the EU attitude towards Britain

The development of intelligence cooperation on law enforcement level among the EU has been a test case for the member states credibility and willingness to deliver their secret assets to a common pool of strategic resources regardless of information security concerns and communication barriers.

There are several opinions that illustrate a clear picture of shallow security approach and mistrust in the field of security on law enforcement level within the European Union member states. Some understand that as the EU law is supreme, therefore, law making process in the UK has weaken, some view the present intelligence cooperation as an insincere and a reluctant engagement, while some understand that the exchange of professional and high quality intelligence information with low quality information of Eastern European states is no more a successful business. However, cooperation on countering terrorism has received shallow support amidst controversies and unwanted statements from some member states. This way of resentment and indignation further prompted social and political clefts in the project infrastructure when some member state expressed deep concern over the reluctant intelligence cooperation.

Intelligence sharing and cooperation on law enforcement level among EU member states is crucial to stability and peace. As movements of EU citizens across borders and volatile regions increases, and groups like Islamic State, domestic radicalized organization and lone wolves have taken roots, trans-border intelligence sharing can prevent any possible terrorist attack. The growing distrust, and dilapidating security situation in Britain and EU is matter of great concern where radicalized groups and lone wolves have established secret cell, recruit young people and carrying attacks against civilian and government installations.

Throughout the 1990s, intelligence cooperation among the EU member states has been very effective and can be seen from the Maastricht Treaty, the Amsterdam Treaty, the St. Petersburg task, and specifically altercation in Gulf, Afghanistan and Bosnia, which showed the European intelligence cooperation with the United States based on strong relationship. Amidst this unfolding security crisis, the Lisbon Treaty indicates that national security is the prerogatives of all member states. In his research paper, Mr. Bjorn Fagersten suggests that uncertainty could be controlled through professional security measures:

> When national governments, and increasingly the European Union, make decision relating to security they do so under condition of uncertainty-who is the enemy, what course of action is most suitable and what long term effects can be envisioned, etc. In an age of hybrid war and threats, this uncertainty is bound to increase. One key element in countering hybrid threats is therefore to reduce the level of uncertainty. This can be facilitated by independent media, strong academia, civil society etc. But government have other means as well as they can employ intelligence agencies to reduce uncertainty in areas where other knowledge producing functions are insufficient.[222]

The issue of free movement across EU became matter of great concern when terrorists availed this opportunity, reaching France, UK and Germany and killed hundreds innocent civilians. During the last six years, there were some legal developments in the United Kingdom dealing with terrorism and radicalization. In October 2010, government published National Security Strategy, which identified terrorism as a precarious threat, and in July 2011, the contest strategy was also published due to the increase in terrorist incidents, and some developments in Asia and Africa. In 2012, Protection of Freedom Act 2012 repealed section 44, search and stop powers. Terrorism prevention and investigation act, communication data bill, justice and security bill, and the use of science and technology to counter terrorism were passed amidst the exponentially growing terror threat in the country. Despite all these legal efforts in countering terrorism on Britain's soil, some segments of society criticized the government efforts and termed it against minorities.

Religious cleric Majid Nawaz (June 2016) argued that intelligence agencies like MI6 and GCHQ are the most competent agencies: "Although French and German intelligence services do theoretically have global reach, they have less intense operational activity than the UK, where in particular the GCHQ is a step ahead of all European signal intelligence agencies. This is the result of Europe's tendency to under-invest in intelligence capabilities since the end of the Second World War. There has also been greater distrust and less tolerance

---

[222] Brexit: UK to Leave Single Market, *BBC* 17 January 2017-04-30Brexit: UK to leave single market

towards intelligence services in continental Europe than in the UK, as can be seen from the German reaction to the Snowden allegations".[223]

His argument is based on sweeping generalization and weak intellectual approach to Intelligence and security in the United Kingdom. There are many thing need to be settled, and many weak points to be addressed with the UK intelligence infrastructure. The intelligence approach of MI6, GCHQ, and MI5 to the social and political trends in society, and domestic security is weak as they have adopted a feeble operational mechanism. However, cooperation on countering terrorism has received shallow support amidst controversies and unwanted statements from some sections in society. This way of resentment and indignation further prompted social and political clefts in the social infrastructure when some member of parliament expressed deep concern over the reluctant cooperation between the police and law enforcement agencies after the London and Manchester attacks. The UK government presented its counter-terrorism and security act 2015 (Amended Bill 2016-17) to Parliament for amendment to manage its own security crisis when the pipeline of the EU intelligence cooperation with the country turned to dust. The bill to repeal provisions in the counter terrorism and security act 2015 requiring teachers, and responsible adults to report extremism and radicalization in educational institutions.

However, The EU bill was also introduced to the British Parliament in January 2017. The Bill powers the Prime Minister to notify, under article 50 (2) of the treaty on European Union, the UK willingness to leave the project, and re-design its own counter terrorism strategy. Part 5 of the act 2015, which received royal assent on 12 February 2015, contains provisions to prevent being drawn into terrorism. In February 2015, The EU council member states agreed on the fight against terrorism based on three pillars; security of the citizens, preventing radicalization and safeguarding value, and better cooperation among all member states. The issue of free movement across EU became matter of great concern when terrorists availed this opportunity, reached France and Germany and killed hundreds innocent civilians.

It is clear that intelligence and law enforcement in some European Union (EU) member states is characterized by variety, being the product of their specific history and culture. The majority of states

[223] *Quilliam's Report*, 19 June 2016

still live in the cold war era, while awareness about national security, intelligence and law enforcement is limited in these states. Literacy rate in some Eastern European states is in shambles, arms and explosive are available in their towns and streets. In Central and Western Europe, some states introduced major reforms in the field of law enforcement and intelligence, but the way their intelligence agencies are operating is not professional due to their consecutive failure to tackle national security threats.

In majority of the EU member states, police and intelligence agencies do not know the actual background of those asylum seekers and immigrants who come from Asia, Africa and the Arab world. More than 90 percent immigrants arriving in EU claimed asylum on fake ID and documents. Terrorists and extremist elements who relinquish their groups come to EU, US and UK and claim asylum on fake ID, but the police and secret agencies are unable to recognize their true face. This inconsideration prompted terrorist attacks in various EU member states, in which innocent civilian and law enforcement personnel were killed. The inner pain of Europol can be realized from its low quality performance and achievement in the fields of intelligence collection and policing.

BREXIT AND THE FREE MARKET

On 29 March 2017, British Prime Minister Theresa May triggered article 50 of the Lisbon Treaty. A letter invoking Article-50 of the Lisbon Treaty was hand-delivered to the President of the EU, Mr. Donald Tusk by the UK Ambassador to the European Union, but experts warned that the UK withdrawal from the project, the future of NATO can also become under threat. After the June 2016 vote for Brexit, the UK now feels the ramifications of its decision, and this decision may possibly cost the country.[224] British Prime Minister also warned in her speech that Brexit can have consequences for her country, but threatened that if the EU leaders failed to reach a comprehensive agreement, cooperation on crime and security may prompt difficulties. In her letter, Theresa May told the President of the EU Union:

> Today, therefore, I am writing to give effect to the democratic decision of the people of the United Kingdom. I hereby notify the European Council in accordance with article 50(2) of the treaty on

---

[224] *The Independent* 29 March 2017

European Union of the United Kingdom's intention to withdraw from the European Union. In addition, in accordance with the same article 50(2) as applies by article 106a of the Treaty Establishing the European Atomic Energy Community, I hereby notify the European Council of the United Kingdom's intension to withdraw from the European Atomic Energy Community. References in this letter to the European Union should therefore be taken to include a reference to the European Atomic Energy Community. This letter sets out the approach of Her Majesty's Government to the discussion we will have about the United Kingdom's departure from the European Union and about the deep and special partnership we hope to enjoy- as your closest friend and neighbor- with the European Union once we leave.[225]

In January 1973, Britain had joined European Economic Community, which later on became the EU. The UK had adopted number of treaties further strengthen the integration process. In 1987, the single European Act prompted the completion of single market process by the end of 1992. In 1993, the EU project was established through the Maastricht Treaty. The Treaties of Amsterdam and Nice were reshaped, and the Lisbon Treaty was renamed in 2009. In 2013, British Prime Minister demanded the negotiation on his country's membership of the EU, while on 17 December 2015; the EU Referendum Act 2015 received the MPs support that made provision for holding the Brexit referendum in UK and Gibraltar in June 2016.

With the Brexit referendum in 2016, and the announcement of the British government to leave the EU, relations between Britain and the EU member states remained under strain due to some provoking statements of both the EU and the UK leadership appeared in newspapers. Prime Minister Theresa May had some irksome words against the attitude of the EU leaders, and warned that her government was preparing to crash out of the EU if could not negotiate a reasonable exit deal. However, the EU leaders warned the Britain cannot access the single market and cannot blackmail them. In a highly anticipated address setting out 12 principles, Theresa May said that single market membership came at the cost of "accepting the four freedoms of goods, capital, services and people"-something which the EU leaders had been clear about since the UK's vote to leave the EU on 23 June 2016. "Being out of the EU but a member of the single market would mean complying with the EU's rules and

---

[225] *The Guardian*, 29 March 2017

regulations that implement those freedoms, without having a vote on what those rules and regulations are", Theresa May said.[226]

Before the promulgation of the Treaty of Lisbon, the EU member states used framework decisions for making policing laws, while after the enforcement of Lisbon treaty, law is being made in the form of directives using decision making process. Britain and the EU member states were engaged in an intense debate over the fate of EU immigration as the graph of crime culminated, and an increasing number of incidents of terrorism, serious organized crime, and hate crime challenged the efforts of law enforcement agencies to tackle the deteriorating security situation in the country. Britain had voted to leave the EU because the project's performance has been very poor in the last few years. On 27 December 2016, Judy Dempsey noted in her Washington Post article: "Europe has been so weakened by the tumultuous events of 2016 that it is left unprepared to deal with the three big foreign policy challenges of 2017. . . ...In 2016, the decision by the British to quit the European Union has robbed Europe of a member state that had a long tradition and experience in security, intelligence-gathering and defense".[227]

In the EU, some states, such as Germany, Romania, Poland, France, civilian intelligence infrastructure tackle domestic and foreign threats, while some states have given to law enforcement agencies intelligence powers to fight against corruption and terrorism. This is not a new story because every state wants to involve intelligence in law enforcement operations, or in the policing. In majority Asian and African states, intelligence is fully involve in law enforcement operations, and led the police in the fight against serious organized crime. The crisis of EU intelligence is irksome due to sectarian and ethnic divide. European intelligence agencies lack the confidence of political parties on their mass surveillance system.

In Germany, intelligence law does not allow Federal Intelligence Service (BND) to support police or involve in policing business, while in Estonia and Latvia, intelligence plays important role in policing communities. Targeted surveillance in all EU states is being conducted on different lines. Intelligence agencies of the member states use surveillance but also give importance to human intelligence. In Brussels, Denmark, Finland, France and Italy targeted

[226] *Sky News*, 17 January 2017
[227] *Washington Post* 27 December 2016

surveillance of groups and individuals has strong roots in socicty. In Netherland, intelligence agencies do not violate the privacy of telephone according to the article 13 (2) of the country's constitution. AIVD focuses its signal intelligence on collection through interception communication.[228]

All these legal, political and administrative restrictions indicate that terrorist organizations have established deep roots in the European Union, where they kill innocent civilians and members of law enforcement agencies. In fact, terrorist and extremist groups in Europe are well-resources and organized viz-a-vis the law enforcement agencies. From 2009–2013, there were 10 failed, foiled or completed attacks carried out by these groups. From 2013 to 2017, terrorist and extremist organizations carried out dozens attacks against civilians and law enforcement personnel. To counter the activities of these groups, the EU member states adopted a series of guide lines to revive radicalization strategy.[229]

The EU Intelligence Centre (EU INTCEN) lacks professional analysis and only rely on publicly available information, which causes misunderstanding among all member states. National intelligence agencies of member states do not share their national secret with each other due their internal rivalries and personal policies of stakeholders. The EU members do not spend enough on intelligence, do not want their interference in politics, and do not want to have an ultimate reliance on intelligence reports regarding national security issues. The issue of information leak and classified analysis is matter of great concern.

The debate about the UK policing and intelligence cooperation with the EU after Brexit is driven more by emotion than by rational analysis. The present trained relations of Britain with European nations and the way they treat each other indicates that cooperation on law enforcement level is cannot be continued. The question that Britain is an intelligence superpower is totally wrong and underwhelming. Intelligence community in Britain is deep professional and operational crisis, and unable to eradicate the roots of terrorism and extremism in the country. The UK intelligence relations have been

---

[228] Surveillance by intelligence services: fundamental rights safeguards and remedies in the EU. Mapping Member States' legal frameworks, European Union Agency for Fundamental Rights, 2015
[229] Ibid.

bilateral but never been friendlier due to some complaints raised by successive British government that European intelligence agencies were incompetent, and their intelligence information has always been of low quality.

Secondly, the UK Home and Foreign offices are of the opinion that the EU law enforcement agencies and intelligence community suffer from number of professional and administrative weaknesses which, if not absent in Britain, are notably less pervasive there. Personal and national interests are also bigger hindrance in their way of mutual cooperation. Some self-styled leaders in Britain and some in European states are making things worse. Their differences start from Iraq, Libya and Afghanistan, where different stake holders misled both sides on the issue of counter terrorism.

The EU looks toward the United States, but in the US it is fashionable to focus attention on Russia and China instead of Europe. Britain also faces deep economic and political crisis due to its abrupt withdrawal from European Union. The idea to established a professional intelligence agency for the EU, all member state are struggling to reach their goal, but reservations of some member states, personal interests, and political differences have made weak their resolve. Experts suggest that EU needs to provide solution to the intelligence information sharing crisis among member states as they do not want to share their national secrets.

Intelligence sharing among as many as 28 member states is not an easy task as it seems that policy makers and secret services face numerous legal, technical and political obstacles. Large states such as France, Germany, and the UK have established significant counter-terrorism institutions and human resources to maintain sophisticated intelligence networks. However, in spite of all these arrangements, terrorists are cruising across Europe with arms and expertise. The limited cooperation on security issues amongst all 28 states is, thus, a reminder that even after six decades of integration, the EU remains a weak project. Intelligence cooperation and adverse relationship between the EU and UK will not cease after the Brexit as the UK contributes a lot in the field of intelligence and law enforcement.

The EU single market is seen by its advocates as a great achievement but the present political and financial ruckus across the continent has put it in danger. The market which was completed in 1992 facilitated free movement of goods and other related materials across Europe but recent borders restrictions and terrorist attacks in some EU member states, the future of single market has become bleak. In February 2017, the Brexit White Paper was available in Internet that elucidates the EU policy and strategy, and explained how Britain can negotiate the area of free trade with the project member states. Britain needs to discuss the issue of free movement of people as 3 million people from all states have already been settled while more are on their way to Britain. Michael Emerson (2017) elucidates the EU immigrants issue and some policy matters relating to the immigration mechanism in the UK:

> Given the unpleasant atmosphere towards EU immigrants created during the referendum campaign, and now the uncertainty surrounding their future status in the UK, it is not surprising that these numbers have declined. Caution is still needed, however, in interpreting these figures since the time series of data is quite erratic. But if this new trend is sustained and possibly amplified, the context of the UK immigration policy is totally changed, calling into question the need for bureaucratically heavy regulations and procedures.[230]

The EU white paper published on 01 March 2017 reflected the Union commitment to a peaceful coexistence. Inspired by a peaceful relationship, the EU started the integration process to peacefully settle mutual differences. The EU kept open the door for new members to join. The union of more than 500 million citizens in 27 independent and sovereign states is committed to prosperity and aggrandizement. During the past two decades, the Treaties of Maastricht, Amsterdam and Nice transformed the EU into a brilliant continent. The present white paper highlights the future goal of member states. On 28 June 2016, EU Council published its Foreign and Security policy coincided with the Britain's decision to leave the project. The introduction and implementation of such a policy came at a time of adverse economic and political crisis of the integration process of European Union.

Major political, economic, and technological developments in the continent and distrust between Britain and the EU project has prompted questionable situation in the trade market of the country, which is very much dependent on imports from European Union. The UK's 58 percent exports go to EU, which is the biggest trade volume in the continent. Germany, Netherlands and France are its

---

[230] *BBC* 16 June 2016

bigger trade partners, while the United State also boosts the UK market by investing billion dollars in various sectors. International trade is undoubtedly, the exchange of capital, products and import and export-related activities across borders, but as is evident from the fact, the UK economy is dependent on foreign trade, for that reason the country is active in a multifaceted trade activities worldwide. There are hundreds largest international trade and investment corporations operating here of which more than 60 belong to the US investors.

John Dudovskiy's recent study spotlights some global impacts on the UK business organization and elucidates that these impacts increase the level of multiculturalism in the country's organizations, and level of interdependency of national economies. The impact of global forces on British market, as he noted are political, economic, social, technological, legal and ecological, while global environment and competitions are the main actors. These factors give us unbelievable understanding of lifestyle patterns and tastes of any population. Law and regulations are factors that can also affect British business strategies where business organizations need to find ways they can react to the change of law affecting their way of business within the EU member states. However, in the EU market, the UK organizations also need to regulate them. Political and global insecurity and weak economic growth are factors that can influence the spending habits of consumers in Europe. The development of transportation and logistics in EU member states played important role in facilitating trade and lowering cost of transportation across Europe. Internet, E-commerce and websites also leave effects on market economy.

The revolving nature of European economy, banking and monetary systems, EU tax rate, money supply system, cash reserve-ratio and fiscal policies can leave the same impact on British market economy. However, market structures in Europe such as perfect competition, monopoly and others can also impact the UK market, if business organizations did not meet marketing standard of every state, because maintain better quality standards, and fixing a reasonable price for the local customers are important requirements of the EU single market. Recently, some legal developments in France and Germany also created difficulties for the UK based business organizations. The new EU security and privacy requirements are important in impacting organizations business data share.

On 23 June 2016, the United Kingdom held referendum which left deep impacts on business industry in both Europe and UK. Now, with this act of the British government, the EU would apply its external customs duties on the UK goods, and it may possibly introduce non-tariff hurdles for goods. However, Brussels can also restrict UK's ability to conduct euro transactions and euro-derivatives transactions, and thereby undermine the position of the City of London as the financial center of the world.

UK citizens may also lose their right of open trade in all EU member states. Moreover, there are many factors of Brexit that can impact the UK based business organizations while some EU member states like Germany, Italy and Spain want integration. The Brexit may also cause political instability in the UK and EU or the collapse of European Union, inflame anti EU sentiments in UK and can empower nationalist and Eurosceptic forces. Brexit would not only be bad for Britain, it will also affect the EU markets. After a successful campaign David Cameron resigned on the pretext that he was against Brexit, while the fact of the matter is, he was behind the whole story, in which he played a crucial role. As a Prime Minister, David Cameron was very upset of the underwhelming attitude of EU leaders. They never allowed him to act independently, and challenged many internal policies of his government. These and other disagreements prompted the withdrawal of Britain from European Union.

Although, majority of the EU members states do not want Britain to have customize relationship with the project, but there is a constant need to limit the fallout of Britain's withdrawal, and to strengthen relationship between the European Union states and Britain. Some statements issued from different political and military circles in Europe and the United Kingdom had misconceptions of the prospect of economic and military prospects in the region. The UK withdrawal from the EU doesn't mean that it will not cooperate with member states on various economic and political issues. The UK needs EU and EU also needs the country's cooperation in countering terrorism, and intelligence sharing on law enforcement level. In 2015, Britain's Strategic and Defense Review stressed that NATO is important for its security, while the country's special relationship with the Unites

States has also been mentioned that connection between the two states on nuclear, security, intelligence, diplomacy, technology and military buildup plays a major role in guaranteeing the UK national security.

CHAPTER 11. THE PROSPECT OF BIOLOGICAL, RADIOLOGICAL, CHEMICAL AND NUCLEAR TERRORISM IN EUROPE AND THE UNITED KINGDOM

The EU internal security strategy was established in 2010 to intensify the fight against terrorism and radicalization. From 2010 to 2014, the strategy was effective, while after 2015, new political and security development in member states prompted security failures. Terrorist groups established networks in the EU, and materials for dirty bomb were openly available in black market. The UK decision to leave EU and election in the US, France, Britain, and Germany added to the list of uncertainties and challenges of the European Council. Domestic security issues and conflict prevention was a priority before ethnic and sectarian war in Balkans, and the EU crisis management systems was not fully recognized.

There were different perceptions in the EU and in the UK about the threat of chemical, biological and radiological terrorism. Terrorist and extremist groups continued to train their members in Iraq and Syria, and use them in European Union States against the government and civilian installations. Many of the chemical and biological weapons could be used in a military way. As we have been experiencing the use of these weapons in some states in Asia, Persian Gulf, South Asia, Middles East and Africa, since a decade, the threat of the use of these weapons existed in all EU member states as ISIL tried to steal nuclear weapons from Brussels during the terrorist attacks. The EU is facing an escalating threat from radicalized elements and foreign sponsored terrorist groups who retrieved expertise in using chemical and biological weapons.

On 22 May 2017, terrorists attacked a concert by an American singer in Manchester city. The attacker was 22-year-old Salman Ramadan Abedi, who detonated a shrapnel-laden homemade bomb at the exit of the arena after the show. Twenty-three adults and children were killed, including Abedi, and 119 were injured. Middle East Eye reported that the British government operated an 'open door' policy that allowed Libyan exiles and British-Libyan citizens to join the 2011 uprising that toppled Muammar Qadafi's regime. According to the Daily Mail report, "When they returned to the UK, having spent months alongside groups thought by British intelligence to have links with Al-Qaeda, rebels were said to have been allowed back into the country without hesitation".[231]

Speaking in Downing Street about the Manchester terror attack, the British Prime Minister said:

> I have just chaired a meeting of the Government's emergency committee Cobra where we discussed the details of and the response to the appalling events in Manchester last night.... Our thoughts and prayers are with the victims and the families and friends of all those affected....It is now beyond doubt that the people of Manchester and of this country have fallen victim to a callous terrorist attack, an attack that targeted some of the youngest people in our society with cold calculation....This was among the worst terrorist incidents we have ever experienced in the United Kingdom and although it is not the first time Manchester has suffered in this way it is the worst attack the city has experienced and the worse ever to hit the north of England.[232]

To identify terrorist and radicalized elements, several European states joined the ranks of 'surveillance states' as new laws allowing indiscriminate mass surveillance have been passed giving intrusive powers to security and intelligence services. Mass surveillance powers have been granted or otherwise expanded in the UK, France, Germany, Poland, Hungary, Austria, Belgium, and the Netherlands, among others, allowing the mass interception of and possible access to the data of millions of people.[233]

On 04 June 2017, terrorists targeted civilians at London Bridge and Borough market killing 6 people and injured more than fifty. The three attackers were shot by armed officers. They were wearing what

---

[231] *Daily Mail*
[232] *Telegraph*, 23 May 2017
[233] *Newsweek*, 17 January 2017

appeared to be explosive vests but were later discovered to be hoaxes. The attackers were Pakistani terrorists. The London Bridge station was shut down and police rapidly sealed off the area. The attack occurred soon after the terrorist threat level had been downgraded from critical to severe. Before these attacks, on 01 January 2017, British Security Minister Ben Wallace warned that the ISIL might use biological and chemical weapons in attacks against civilians. "They have no moral objection to using chemical weapons against populations and if they could, they would in this country. "The casualty figures which could be involved would be everybody's worst fear. "We have certainly seen reports of them using it in Syria and Iraq [and] we have certainly seen aspiration for it in Europe."[234]

Countering nuclear terrorism is an international partnership that was launched by the United States and the Russian Federation in July 2006, for the purpose of intercepting biological and nuclear weapons falling into wrong hands. The convention of chemical weapons, in fact, a disarmament convention for intercepting the production of chemical weapons. There have been several episodes, which have been reported in the media over the past three years, from the seizure of liquid radioactive waste at Mosul University.

As any international institution trying to deal with such a big problem as WMD counter proliferation, especially as regards to non state actors, they always face some sort of legitimacy challenge. In all 27 EU member states, more than 143 nuclear reactors are in operation and more reactors are under construction. Increased awareness of the risks posed by mass impact terrorism has underlined the fact that reactors represent a potential vulnerability as well as being an asset. And now experts have said the jihadi death cult are looking to develop nuclear weapons that mark the biggest threat to Europe since the cold war. Moshe Kantor, head of the Luxembourg Forum on Preventing Nuclear Catastrophe, warned: "ISIS has already carried out numerous chemical weapons attacks in Syria".

In his Time Magazine article, Mr. Simon Shuster warned about the threat of dirty bomb use by terrorist organizations: "The lasting effects of a dirty bomb make this weapon especially attractive to terrorists. Fear of contamination would drive away tourists and customers, and cleanup would be costly: the economic impact could be worse than

---

[234] 01 January 2017, British Security Minister Ben Wallace warned that the ISIL might use biological and chemical weapons in attacks against civilians.

that of the attacks of 9/11, according to a study conducted in 2004 by the National Defense University. "It would change our world," President Obama said of a potential dirty bomb in April 2016. "We cannot be complacent." However, in May 2015, Islamic state claimed that it can purchase a nuclear device on the black market—and to "pull off something truly epic." The threat of a 'dirty bomb' terror attack on a European city is at its highest level since the end of the Cold War, international nuclear experts have warned. ISIS's efforts to obtain nuclear materials, and continued threats to attack Western capitals contribute to experts' analysis that the threat of a bomb is higher than ever".[235]

However, Middle East News quoted the EU Report about the ISIS use of Chemical or Biological weapons in West: "Terrorist group already has foreign fighters on its payroll who can manufacture lethal weapons from raw materials, as well as access to toxic agents left behind by the tyrants of Syria, Iraq and Libya. In June 2014, ISIS seized control of Muthanna, Iraq, once the Saddam Hussein regime's primary chemical-weapons production facility". On 05 April 2017, the Guardian reported the ISIL chemical attacks in Syria, in which 70 civilians were killed. The US President Donald Trump denounced the carnage as a "heinous" act that "cannot be ignored by the civilized world". But he also laid some of the responsibility on Barack Obama, saying in a statement that the attack was "a consequence of the past administration's weakness and irresolution". The Newspaper reported.[236]

In June 2005, Oxford Research Group published a comprehensive article of DR. Frank Barnaby who elucidated the fatalities of dirty bomb and warned that material of the bomb is easily available:

> A dirty bomb is not the same as a nuclear weapon in the normal sense of the phrase since it does not involve a nuclear explosion. Many types of radioisotopes (radioactive isotopes) could be used in a dirty bomb. The most likely to be used is one that is that is relatively easily available, has a relatively long half-life, and emits energetic radiation. . . . .The use of plutonium in a dirty bomb would cause the greatest threat to human health, because of its very high inhalation toxicity, and the most extensive contamination. . . . .The detonation

---

[235] Inside the Uranium Underworld: Dark Secrets, Dirty Bombs, Simon Shuster, *Time Magazine*, 10 April 2017.

[236] On 05 April 2017, *the Guardian* reported the ISIL chemical attacks in Syria, in which 70 civilians were killed. The US President Donald Trump denounced the carnage as a "heinous" act that "cannot be ignored by the civilised world".

of a dirty bomb is likely to result in some deaths but would not result in the hundreds of thousands of fatalities that could be caused by the explosion in a city of a crude nuclear weapon. Generally, the explosion of the conventional explosive would be the most likely cause of any immediate deaths or serious injuries. The radioactive material in the bomb would be dispersed into the air but would be soon diluted to relatively low concentrations.[237]

The Guardian reported Prime Minister Theresa May expressed concern and said she was appalled by reports of the attack and called for an investigation by the Organization for the Prohibition of Chemical Weapons. "I'm very clear that there can be no future for Assad in a stable Syria which is representative of all the Syrian people and I call on all the third parties involved to ensure that we have a transition away from Assad. We cannot allow this suffering to continue," she said. However, Europol in its report warned that Islamic State can carry out terrorist attacks in the EU, Europol warns, citing intelligence sources. Jihadists may resort to tactics that they use in Syria and Iraq, such as car bombs, extortion and kidnappings, according to a new report".[238]

A report in the Journal of Environmental Protection and Ecology defined the threat of biological and nuclear weapons:

> Chemical, biological, radiological and nuclear (CBRN) weapons pose the one of the most serious threats to the SEEC and their foreign interests. Ballistic and cruise missiles, aircraft, covert forces, and terrorist groups are considered possible means of delivering these weapons of mass destruction. The total number of chemical, biological, radiological and nuclear weapons stockpiled throughout the world is decreasing as the major powers scale back their inventories, but some additional countries and groups are trying to acquire these weapons. The EU and SEEC and allied policy-makers debate the rate of proliferation and the nature and extent of the threat to the EU–SEEC and their allies, and the weapons effects on international stability. These issues and the policy preferences of various segments of the security policy communities in the SEEC and overseas have led to markedly different approaches to countering CBRN weapons and missile threats. The purpose of this paragraph is to assemble compendiously current information on the status of

---

[237] Bombs and Primitive Nuclear Weapons Dr. Frank Barnaby, Oxford Research Group, June 2005
[238] Ibid.

weapons programs around the globe and analyze patterns regarding the threats posed by these weapons.[239]

Moldova has become the center of dirty bomb material smugglers where they sell nuclear and biological materials in open markets. One article warned in particularly stark terms that traffickers are moving radioactive materials through Moldova:

> In one investigation in Chisinau, Moldova, samples of uranium-235 and cesium-135 were seized by police when a smuggler offered an informant who was posing as a buyer for ISIS enough cesium to contaminate several city blocks—and all for $2.5 million. An in-depth investigation into dirty bombs by the Associated Press revealed four other attempts by criminal networks to traffic radioactive materials through Moldova. Last spring, in a New York federal court, another perpetrator, this time a Colombian national, was convicted for obtaining enriched uranium with the purpose of supplying a South American–based terrorist group with a dirty bomb to attack U.S. military personnel or a U.S. embassy.[240]

However, the CNBC International report (Feb 2016) warned that the recovery of chemical and biological weapons from Basra needs the attention of international community: "material, stored in a protective case the size of a laptop computer, went missing from a storage facility near the southern city of Basra belonging to U.S. oilfield services company Weatherford, an environment ministry document seen by Reuters showed and security, environmental and provincial officials confirmed. A spokesman for Iraq's environment ministry said he could not discuss the issue, citing national security concerns. Weatherford said in a statement that it was not responsible or liable for the theft. "We do not own, operate or control sources or the bunker where the sources are stored," it said. CNBC reported.[241]

On 19 February 2016, the Independent newspaper reported Islamic State (ISIL) was monitoring the Belgian nuclear scientist during his professional activities. "After the Brussels terrorist attacks, the Belgian police seized surveillance footage of the high-ranking nuclear official-who had not been identified for security reasons. Investigators

---

[239] In *Journal of Environmental Protection and Ecology* (2010), M. Chalarisa P. and Stavrakakisb, P. Sarafisc have defined the threat of biological and nuclear weapons

[240] "The Dirty Bomb Threat Too Dangerous to Do Nothing," Pamela S. Falk, *Foreign Affairs*, 04 April , 2017

[241] Islamic State could use stolen radioactive material for dirty bomb: Iraqi official, *CNBC*, 18 Feb 2016

speculated that the suspects intended to kidnap the official, who had access to secure areas of a nuclear research facility in Mol-potentially to gain access to the facility and acquire enough radioactive material to create a dirty bomb. Interior Minister Jan Jambon told Belgium's Parliament the ministry determined there was a threat "to the person in question, but not the nuclear facilities".[242]

Moreover, Paul Cornish in his report for International Security Programme (February 2007) warned that these weapons are dangerous to human life: "Chemical weapons have a long history of research, development and production for use on the battlefield. But in the environment of the battlefield, the effect and therefore utility of CW have to a considerable extent been neutered through training and preparation, and through the provision of protection and decontamination equipment, and antidotes..........In such an environment, the public (and therefore the democratic political elite which responds to public concerns) would be unlikely to sense much more than the narrowest of margins for optimism, escape or recovery. The lethality of CW (particularly nerve agents such as sarin) is widely perceived to be so extreme, the availability of CW (or TIH) so widespread, and the vulnerability of any single, unprotected person so complete, that the working assumption in the public/political mind is that the use of chemical agents against an open target is both possible and certain to lead to near-instant death for its victims".[243]

The exponentially growing threat of chemical attacks by lone wolves is tenaciously realized in Europe while misunderstanding between the EU member states has put joint anti terror mechanism in procrastination. The overall threat to security increased with the arrival of ISIL trained lone wolves in Europe. In November 2015, attacks in Paris, and terror attacks in Copenhagen, London, Manchester, Denmark, and the knife attack in Nice, France underscore the diversity of the threat. Threat of nuclear, chemical and biological terrorism is causing deep concern and anxiety within the European Union member states and the United Kingdom, since cases of nuclear smuggling have been reported by local and international media in Europe. Intelligence and law enforcement agencies of member states

---

[242] On 19 February 2016 *the Independent newspaper* reported Islamic State (ISIL) was monitoring the Belgian nuclear scientist during his professional activities.
[243] Paul Cornish in his report for International Security Programme (February 2007) warned that these weapons are dangerous to human life

successfully arrested several people linked to nuclear smuggling in some states, and recovered explosive material in small and large quantities. These arrests prompted deep concern in civil society that lone wolves or extremist citizens of the EU member states can resort to nuclear, chemical, radiological and biological attacks. In his research analysis, Glancarlo Elia Valori (2016) also noted the threat of dirty bomb use in the EU. He also limelighted the ISIL monitoring of Belgian scientist who operated in Dohel:

> On November 30, 2015 the Belgian police discovered a film regarding the movements of a Belgian nuclear researcher and his family who operated in Dohel-1, one of the seven nuclear production sites in that country, four in the Dohel region and three in the Tihange region. The long film of all the nuclear expert's movements was found in the Auvelais house of a man linked to the network of Al Baghdadi's Caliphate. The jihadists were interested not so much in the nuclear plant as such, but in the possibility of using radioisotopes, namely products capable of causing poisonings, diseases, and various temporary or permanent disorders in those who come into contact with them for a certain period of time. Radioisotopes, also known as radionuclides, are unstable nuclei which radioactively decay, resulting in the emission of nuclear radiations. As already said, the effects may be scarcely or highly significant, depending on the dose of radiations received and/or the type of emissions absorbed.[244]

Some dissident groups like New IRA, ISIL and local extremist and radicalized groups can easily retrieve nuclear and chemical weapons from Eastern European black market as they have established strong links with nuclear smugglers. The availability of nuclear explosive material and enriched uranium in some Eastern European states like Moldova, Lithuania, and Georgia, and secret efforts of some groups and individuals for nuclear material delivery to the Islamic State (ISIL), and other violent groups has put in danger the stability and security of the entire region. Terrorist groups in Northern Ireland used variety of Improvised Explosive Devices and grenades against the police and other forces, but they couldn't succeed in this campaign. In the UK and in the EU, homemade explosive device can be easily constituted in many ways as it is cheap and its material is available in open market. There are speculations that terrorist and extremist

---

[244] The "dirty bomb" issue and the jihadist strategy in Europe, Glancarlo Elia Valori , *Modern Diplomacy*, 01 April, 2016,http://moderndiplomacy.eu/index.php?option=com_k2&view=item&id=1327:the-dirty-bomb-issue-and-the-jihadist-strategy-in-europe&Itemid=488

groups retrieved more expert knowhow in making this device. The Europol Report for 2016 warned:

> The transfer of knowledge to the EU has been facilitated by the phenomenon of foreign terrorist fighters and returnees. There are indications that some of the fighters in the conflict zones have received advance training in manufacturing and using in IEDs. Moreover, recent investigations show that certain terrorist groups continue to establish large stockpiles of explosive precursors in the EU in order to manufacture HMEs. The key to managing the risk of CBRN weapons used by non-state actors is to recognize that the threat is dynamic, not static; the relative rarity of past events mean that historical trends may not provide reliable indicators on the current and future risk. The expertise and capacity to use chemical weapons on the battlefield of Syria and Iraq could be used to plan attacks outside these regional conflicts in the near future. The deliberate contamination of water supplies is seen as a plausible CBRN scenario. A few day after the November 13th terrorist attacks in Paris, a number of proactive suits, gloves and masks used to protect individuals from exposure to biological contaminants, were reported missing from a locked room in a hospital in Paris.[245]

Criminal, extremist and terrorist groups in EU and the United Kingdom may possibly carry out chemical, biological, or nuclear attacks to create consternation and security crisis. However, States and criminal groups seeking nuclear explosive materials and terror-related technologies to use it against their rivals, have no difficulties in retrieving uranium and radioactive material as well. As the threat of nuclear terrorism is evolving, cyber-attacks, nuclear, chemical and biological terrorism, can inflict huge fatalities on civilian population in the region. From Lithuania to Georgia and Moldova, terrorist groups are striving to retrieve nuclear material and use it against their target. In these circumstances, the United Kingdom and EU member states are under precarious threat from lone wolves, ISIL returnees and local radicalized groups.

The threat of nuclear, biological and chemical terrorism is intensified in the region while terrorist and radicalized groups in Europe are struggling to obtain biological and nuclear weapon by making links with local experts working in nuclear sites. After the Brussels attacks police found links between terrorists and insider to attack nuclear installations. The Europol Report for 2016 highlighted

---

[245] *Europol*: European Union Terrorism Situation and Trends Report 2016

the availability and theft of radioactive sources and trafficking of weapons of mass destruction in European market:

> In 2015 for example, two incidents involving the theft of radioactive sources, which are commonly used in various authorized applications in industry, medicine and research, were reported by Poland. Nevertheless, there were no reported cases of radioactive materials being used to deliberately injure or poison people. In the European Union, trafficking cases are rare because nuclear and other radioactive materials are relatively well safeguarded, both by regulation and enforcement. However, in EU neighboring former Soviet Union countries, nuclear and radioactive materials have continued to appear on the black market since the early 1990s. In 2015 incidents involving the attempted sale of radioactive materials by organized crime groups occurred in Moldova, Ukraine and Turkey. Although there is no information on potential links between the groups involved in these three cases and terrorist organizations, criminals, with access to these materials can potentially play a role in acquiring and selling radioactive materials to terrorist groups? The procurement of biological toxins such as Abrin and ricin has been reported as taking place in underground marketplaces on the Darknet, on occasion using virtual currencies.[246]

As the threat of biological and chemical terrorism has intensified, the United Kingdom and Europe have adopted several preventive measures and strategies to prevent these weapons falling into the hands of ISIL and other radicalized groups. The London, Brussels, Germany and France attacks jolted the whole Europe while terrorists also strived to obtain chemical and nuclear weapons from Brussels but failed. Presently all modern states are vulnerable to massive loss of life from an attack involving a weapon of mass destruction — nuclear, biological or chemical (NBC). Moreover, there is a danger that these weapons may possibly fall into the hands of terrorist groups based in Europe and the UK, in order to use against the police and armed forces. There are reports, in which scientists have warned that 'tomorrow's threat may include the use of chemicals, bacteriological agents, radioactive materials and even nuclear technology. Terrorist groups are trying to develop dirty bombs, and the possibilities of a catastrophic terrorist attack against many countries are growing and security at many of country's civil nuclear facilities remains insufficient.

---

[246] Ibid.

The possibility of terrorist use of Improvised Explosive Device cannot be ruled out as these groups have already used these weapons in some states. An IED is a bomb fabricated in an improvised manner incorporating destructive, lethal, noxious, pyrotechnic, or incendiary chemicals and designed to destroy or incapacitate personnel or vehicles. All European states are under threat from their domestic radicalized groups. These groups have developed expertise in making dirty bomb. The number of chemical, biological, stockpiled in EU member states is in increase as the major powers scale back their inventories, but some additional countries and groups are trying to acquire these weapons. Recent attacks in the United States have created fear that terrorist may possibly use biological and nuclear weapons in their attacks against civilians. Because chemical, biological, material as well as industrial agents can be dispersed in the air we breathe, the water we drink, or on surfaces we physically contact.

If they used these weapons, the whole scenario of countering chemical and biological terrorism might change, and it is possible that national armies may come out to fight these groups in streets and markets. In European states, the UK and Middle East, terrorist and radicalized groups could construct improvised but effective biological weapons. Retrieving pathogenic Microorganisms is not a difficult task for these organizations, but one easy way is to obtain biological weapons. Moreover, there are possibilities that terrorist groups may prefer to buy radiological and nuclear weapons instead or developing a dirt bomb. If states that support terrorism purvey or sell a nuclear device to terrorist groups, they may also put at stake the security of its own nuclear assets.

Though, the intelligence and law enforcement agencies of the EU member states have developed tools and expertise to recognize and interdict nuclear attacks, but technological development and expertise of terrorist groups in making complicated nuclear explosive device cannot be easily detected. In previous chapters, I analyzed and spotlighted the weaknesses and challenges of the EU intelligence agencies during the last five years, when terrorists succeeded in carrying out attacks in towns and cities of Brussels, London, Germany, Sweden and France. The threat of lone wolves is more complicated. Lone wolves can be hired, recruited and used for nuclear or biological attacks by terrorist organization both in the EU and Britain. If this link is developed and he/she is recruited then law enforcement and intelligence agencies will suffer deep and an unending ordeal. Trafficking nuclear and biological material have been recognized in the EU member states as a precarious threat to national security, policing, counter-terrorism agencies and national critical infrastructure.

The free movement of people across the EU vulnerable and mismanaged borders on daily bases, and the free movement of terrorist and criminal mafia groups across the continent, can cause major terror attacks. Terrorists and experts of improvised explosive devices, or chemical bomb easily enter the UK and European Union by train, by air and via sea as they are already in contact with local terrorist and extremist organizations. This illegal movement cannot be stopped as traffickers have developed clandestine relationship with local traffickers and insiders in Europe who provides them with shelter and other facilities.

The EU non-proliferation consortium in its non-proliferation paper no-39 has noted important incidents of nuclear smuggling within the EU member states: "As people, both inside and outside the nuclear sector, sought new ways to make a living, or in some cases a fortune, some individual began to explore illegal trade in nuclear material and the first successful theft of uranium and plutonium occurred. As a result the countries in Eastern and Central Europe experienced a wave of nuclear trafficking from the former Soviet Union. Arrests of criminal trying to smuggle or sell nuclear material were frequently reported by Austria, the Czech Republic, Germany, Hungary, Poland, and other European countries, thus creating the impression that a nuclear black market existed in Europe".[247]

The construction of chemical bomb is nor as difficult for radicalized groups as they have developed expertise. Radiological and chemical material is accessible and can be obtained from black market. The material can even be lurked in a suitcase. The Dirty bombs have the potential to cause panic and massive economic costs. In Norway, on 22 July 2011, a lone actor, Mr. Anders Behring Breivik killed 77 innocent civilians. In their literature review about the 'Lone –Actor

---

[247] EU Non-Proliferation Consortium, No-39 Nuclear Trafficking Issue in the Black Sea Region. Lyudmila Zaitseva and Friedrich Steinhausler

Terrorism' Raffaello Pantucci, Clare Ellis and Lorien Chaplais have spotlighted some vulnerable aspects of a lone wolf:

Policy-makers and practitioners across Europe have recognized the prominent place of lone actors in the current terrorist-threat landscape; however, considerable obstacles remain in effectively countering the threat. Acting in isolation without guidance, communications or potentially any interaction with a wider-group, lone actors present acute difficulties in detection and disruption. Furthermore, it is not always clear that lone actors are truly alone, and usually investigation uncovers contacts, leakage and evidence of connection with others that casts doubt on the degree of isolation that can be attributed to an individual. Research has an important role in providing insights into this threat and its likely manifestation, and can make a particularly strong contribution as the threat continues to evolve through its interaction with the phenomenon of foreign fighters travelling to Syria and Iraq. However, before undertaking research in this area it is important to understand the state of the current literature, where significant gaps remain, and what can be learned from the application of different methodologies.[248]

Now Europe is facing the threat of lone wolves as they have already carried out attacks in Paris, Germany and Britain. There has never been higher numbers of attack plots per year than in 2014-16. An increasing proportion of plots goes undetected and result in deadly attacks. Richard A Falkenrath, Robert D Newman, Bradley argued that the ISIL in its international operations and in EU generated talk of new trends in modus operandi, perpetrator profiles and radicalization.

In their well-written book, (America's Achilles' Heel: Nuclear, Biological, and Chemical Terrorism and Covert Attack-1998), Richard A Falkenrath, Robert D Newman, Bradley A Thayer argued that an attack on a crowded indoor area might kill a few thousand people. Some chemical warfare agents are highly persistent, and could render large areas uninhabitable for extended periods of time, requiring costly decontamination and clean-up efforts. They warned that chemical weapons suitable for mass-casualty attacks can be acquired

---

[248] Lone-Actor Terrorism: Literature Review, RaffaelloPantucci, Clare Ellis and LorienChaplais, Royal United Services Institute for Defense and Security Studies London.

by virtually all states and by non-state actors with moderate technical skills.[249]

Scholars Stephanie E. Meulenbelt and Maarten S. Nieuwenhuizen in their research paper have noted the recent use of chemical and biological weapons by the ISIL in Syria and Iraq and the fatalities of weapons of mass destruction in the region. They also focused on the possible use of radiological and biological weapons by non-state actor:

> Recent developments in Syria and its neighboring countries have revitalized awareness of the threat of attacks involving chemical, biological, radiological or nuclear (CBRN) weapons or weapons of mass destruction (WMD). Within this threat, which has historically included conventional use (that is, use in State versus State conflicts), there is a steadily growing concern about the potential use of these weapons by non-State actors. There are increasing indications that certain types of non-State groups have planned or are planning to carry out attacks using CBRN weapons. In relation to Syria, for example, claims of rebels using chemicals, including sarin, in furtherance of their goals have been made. Islamic State (IS) specifically has been accused of using low-grade chemical weapons on several occasions, including chlorine and mustard gas against Kurdish fighters on a number of occasions in 2015. Some argue that the perception of the probability/possibility of CBRN attacks by non-State actors may be different from the real probability as a result of sensationalism or fear.[250]

In 2016, the ISIL terrorists attacked Turkey, Paris, Tunis and Egypt, in which more than 500 people were killed. What motivated him and why he killed these people, the final report of his action is still in limbo. Researchers Brynjar Lia and Petter Nesser described recent developments in EU as a precarious threat to national security: "European Jihadism has clearly had certain geographical points of gravity, London being a main hub. Even if Jihadi networks in Europe have always been transnational in nature with numerous nodes in many countries, the terrorism threat emanating from European

---

[249] America's Achilles' Heel: Nuclear, Biological, and Chemical Terrorism and Covert Attack-1998, Richard A Falkenrath, Robert D Newman, Bradley A Thayer
[250] Non-State actors 'pursuit of CBRN weapons: From motivation to potential humanitarian consequences. Stephanie E. Meulenbelt and Maarten S. Nieuwenhuizen, International Review of the Red Cross (2015). The human cost of nuclear weapons.

Jihadism has historically been much greater in places like Paris, Brussels or London, than in Oslo".[251]

In 2015 police in Moldova stopped four attempts by nuclear smugglers to provide nuclear material to extremist organizations in the Middle East. Associated Press reported a fresh case in February 2015. On 07 October 2015, Associated Press reported some former secret agents of some states were founded involved in the smuggling of nuclear smuggling. The report spotlighted illegal activities of some outlaw individuals and groups involved in nuclear smuggling and enriched uranium. Researchers Sharon Squassoni and Amelia Armitage in their paper noted some weaknesses and corruption of some EU intelligence and law enforcement agencies:

> In locations where governance and rule of law are weak, illicit activities tend to thrive, and illegal sales of nuclear and radioactive materials are no exception. Corruption, organized crime and nuclear material are a dangerous mix. Reported cases of nuclear smuggling soared in the immediate aftermath of the collapse of the Soviet Union in the mid-1990s as a result of lax security and a bad economy. There are some indications that material that entered the black market then may still be for sale today. In addition to Moldova, most states in the Black Sea region have had similar cases-including Georgia, Ukraine, Kazakhstan, and Tajikistan.[252]

Recent cases in which terrorist groups were trying to smuggle cesium — a highly radioactive material could be used in a dirty bomb. These cases in Eastern Europe caused deep consternation within local communities. In most cases in Eastern European states, the authorities responsible for keeping nuclear material secure were weakened or disbanded during the counter-revolutions that returned communist states to the capitalist model, where nuclear smugglers easily got hold of it, as everything is for sale.

The Independent newspaper reported:

> For strategic reasons, in most of the operations arrests were made after samples of nuclear material had been obtained rather than the larger quantities. That means that if smuggler did have access to the bulk of material they offered, it remains in criminal hands. The repeated attempts to peddle radioactive materials signal that a thriving nuclear black market has emerged in an impoverished

---

[251] Researchers Brynjar Lia and PetterNesser describe recent developments in EU
[252] Nuclear Smuggling from Moldova to ISIS? Sharon Squassoni, Amelia Armtage, Centre for Strategic and International Studies, 09 October 2015

corner of Eastern Europe on the fringes of the former Soviet Union. Moldova, which borders Romania, is a former Soviet republic. Moldova police and judicial authorities shared investigative case files with Associated Press in an effort to spotlight how dangerous the black market has become.[253]

As the cases of nuclear smuggling raised concern within the EU member states, intelligence and nuclear counter-terrorism forces expedited efforts to save the continent from abrupt nuclear and biological attacks. On 08 July 2016, Eurasia's Weekly Digest reported: "Three Armenians and three Georgians were detained on April 17 and accused of trying to sell uranium 238 for $200 million in the Georgian capital, Tbilisi.

After the disintegration of the Soviet Union, and the emergence of terrorist and nuclear mafia groups, businesses of nuclear smuggling flourished. Unemployed former KGB and Eastern European intelligence agents had no sources of income to survive, so they entered a dangerous and a profitable business of nuclear, radiological and biological weapons smuggling markets. On 23 September 2015, in his Modern Diplomacy paper, Norberto Morales Rosa noted some important aspects of nuclear black marker:

> Illicit nuclear materials have been interdicted on numerous occasions in Russia, the Caucasus, and Central Asia. If seizures are an accurate indication, most material on the nuclear black market has been of FSU or Eastern European origin. The region's porous borders, government instability, and endemic corruption provide fertile ground for trafficking of WHD materials. This may be partly due to the heavy drug trafficking across the region, which provides a smuggling infrastructure useful for other illicit items.[254]

On 13 November 2015, while footage of Belgian nuclear official was discovered of a terrorist involved in Paris attacks, it exacerbated the concerns of local law enforcement agencies in EU member states. The EU leadership and the United States expressed deep concern on the nuclear weapons falling in the hands of terrorist organization and local extremist groups. As mentioned earlier, lone wolves, terrorist, and extremist group in the EU member states are seeking biological and nuclear weapons to use them against the government and civilian installations. On 30 September 2016, Jean Bernard Latortue in the

---

[253] *Independent newspaper* 07 October 2015
[254] Radioactive: Illicit Materials-Trafficking Across the Greater Caspian, Norberto Morales Rosa, 23 September 2015

International Affairs Review analysis spotlighted the cases of nuclear theft and nuclear weapons smuggling:

> Since an improvised nuclear bomb can be made from highly enriched uranium or plutonium, a terrorist group would not need to take over a nuclear-armed state to posses such a weapon? A thriving black market exists for just materials a terrorist would need to create a bomb on his or her own. As of December 2015, the Internal Atomic Energy Agency Incident and Trafficking Database system has recorded a total of 2889 incidents involving theft, losses, and attempts to illegally sell or traffic fissile materials across international borders. Therefore, a terrorist attack involving an improvised nuclear device is neither inconceivable nor impossible, although it may be improbable. Currently, the International Atomic Energy Agency (IAEA) does not inspect every nuclear facility globally, thus some countries may not be in accordance with the agency's safeguards and nuclear security measures. Even more striking is that states sometimes fail to account for the totality of the nuclear material at their various facilities. For instance, in Pakistan, missing-weapon useable materials are rarely reported by the facility and subsequently turn up on the black market.[255]

The availability of nuclear explosive materials in the black markets of Eastern European states raised serious concern in international community that if these materials are obtained by terrorist organizations and local radicalized groups in Europe, it will endanger the national security of the entire region. No doubt, several European states have taken professional measure in tackling such incidents, but mistrust, inconsideration and lack of intelligence sharing on law enforcement level are causes that prevent them to join hands against nuclear black marketing. On 03 March 2017, in her article published in Global Risk Insight, researcher Orsolya Raczovab outlines the background and possibilities of biological and nuclear weapons falling in the hands of terrorist organization:

> It is relatively easy to obtain information on producing chemical weapons through open source information. Yet the synthesis itself is technologically demanding and often producing toxic side products. Moreover, the deadliest chemical are also the most difficult to manufacture. Nerve agents, including VX and Sarin, are manufactured from precursors that are difficult to obtain, while the synthesis and dispersal requires expertise and special equipment.

[255] Nuclear Weapons and Terrorism: A Dangerous Mix, Jean-Bernard Latortue, *International Affairs Review*, The Elliot Scholl of International Affairs, George Washington University, 30 September 2016

The only partially successful chemical terrorist attacks targeting civilians on a mass-scale were carried out by the wealthy Japanese cult Aum Shinrikyo in the 1990s, aiming to reach civilians on the Tokyo underground.[256]

---

[256] Global Risk Insight, researcher OrsolyaRaczovab, 03 March 2017

A letter invoking Article 50 of the Lisbon Treaty was hand-delivered to the President of the EU, Mr. Donald Tusk, by the UK Ambassador to the European Union on 29 March 2017. It read,

1. On 23 June last year, the people of the United Kingdom voted to leave the European Union. As I have said before, that decision was no rejection of the values we share as fellow Europeans. Nor was it an attempt to do harm to the European Union or any of the remaining member states. On the contrary, the United Kingdom wants the European Union to succeed and prosper. Instead, the referendum was a vote to restore, as we see it, our national self-determination. We are leaving the European Union, but we are not leaving Europe — and we want to remain committed partners and allies to our friends across the continent.

2. Earlier this month, the United Kingdom Parliament confirmed the result of the referendum by voting with clear and convincing majorities in both of its Houses for the European Union (Notification of Withdrawal) Bill. The Bill was passed by Parliament on 13 March and it received Royal Assent from Her Majesty the Queen and became an Act of Parliament on 16 March.

3. Today, therefore, I am writing to give effect to the democratic decision of the people of the United Kingdom. I hereby notify the European Council in accordance with Article 50(2) of the Treaty on European Union of the United Kingdom's intention to withdraw

from the European Union. In addition, in accordance with the same Article 50(2) as applied by Article 106a of the Treaty Establishing the European Atomic Energy Community, I hereby notify the European Council of the United Kingdom's intention to withdraw from the European Atomic Energy Community. References in this letter to the European Union should therefore be taken to include a reference to the European Atomic Energy Community.

4. This letter sets out the approach of Her Majesty's Government to the discussions we will have about the United Kingdom's departure from the European Union and about the deep and special partnership we hope to enjoy — as your closest friend and neighbor — with the European Union once we leave. We believe that these objectives are in the interests not only of the United Kingdom but of the European Union and the wider world too.

5. It is in the best interests of both the United Kingdom and the European Union that we should use the forthcoming process to deliver these objectives in a fair and orderly manner, and with as little disruption as possible on each side. We want to make sure that Europe remains strong and prosperous and is capable of projecting its values, leading in the world, and defending itself from security threats. We want the United Kingdom, through a new deep and special partnership with a strong European Union, to play its full part in achieving these goals. We therefore believe it is necessary to agree the terms of our future partnership alongside those of our withdrawal from the European Union.

6. The Government wants to approach our discussions with ambition, giving citizens and businesses in the United Kingdom and the European Union — and indeed from third countries around the world — as much certainty as possible, as early as possible.

7. I would like to propose some principles that may help to shape our coming discussions, but before I do so, I should update you on the process we will be undertaking at home, in the United Kingdom.

The process in the United Kingdom

8. As I have announced already, the Government will bring forward legislation that will repeal the Act of Parliament — the European Communities Act 1972 — that gives effect to EU law in our country. This legislation will, wherever practical and appropriate, in effect convert the body of existing European Union law (the "acquis") into UK law. This means there will be certainty for UK citizens and

for anybody from the European Union who does business in the United Kingdom. The Government will consult on how we design and implement this legislation, and we will publish a White Paper tomorrow. We also intend to bring forward several other pieces of legislation that address specific issues relating to our departure from the European Union, also with a view to ensuring continuity and certainty, in particular for businesses. We will of course continue to fulfill our responsibilities as a member state while we remain a member of the European Union, and the legislation we propose will not come into effect until we leave.

9. From the start and throughout the discussions, we will negotiate as one United Kingdom, taking due account of the specific interests of every nation and region of the UK as we do so. When it comes to the return of powers back to the United Kingdom, we will consult fully on which powers should reside in Westminster and which should be devolved to Scotland, Wales and Northern Ireland. But it is the expectation of the Government that the outcome of this process will be a significant increase in the decision-making power of each devolved administration.

Negotiations between the United Kingdom and the European Union

10. The United Kingdom wants to agree with the European Union a deep and special partnership that takes in both economic and security cooperation. To achieve this, we believe it is necessary to agree the terms of our future partnership alongside those of our withdrawal from the EU.

11. If, however, we leave the European Union without an agreement the default position is that we would have to trade on World Trade Organization terms. In security terms a failure to reach agreement would mean our cooperation in the fight against crime and terrorism would be weakened. In this kind of scenario, both the United Kingdom and the European Union would of course cope with the change, but it is not the outcome that either side should seek. We must therefore work hard to avoid that outcome.

12. It is for these reasons that we want to be able to agree a deep and special partnership, taking in both economic and security cooperation, but it is also because we want to play our part in making sure that Europe remains strong and prosperous and able to lead in the world, projecting its values and defending itself from security

threats. And we want the United Kingdom to play its full part in realizing that vision for our continent.

PROPOSED PRINCIPLES FOR OUR DISCUSSIONS

13. Looking ahead to the discussions which we will soon begin, I would like to suggest some principles that we might agree to help make sure that the process is as smooth and successful as possible.

14. We should engage with one another constructively and respectfully, in a spirit of sincere cooperation. Since I became Prime Minister of the United Kingdom I have listened carefully to you, to my fellow EU Heads of Government and the Presidents of the European Commission and Parliament. That is why the United Kingdom does not seek membership of the single market: we understand and respect your position that the four freedoms of the single market are indivisible and there can be no "cherry picking". We also understand that there will be consequences for the UK of leaving the EU: we know that we will lose influence over the rules that affect the European economy. We also know that UK companies will, as they trade within the EU, have to align with rules agreed by institutions of which we are no longer a part — just as UK companies do in other overseas markets.

15. We should always put our citizens first. There is obvious complexity in the discussions we are about to undertake, but we should remember that at the heart of our talks are the interests of all our citizens. There are, for example, many citizens of the remaining member states living in the United Kingdom, and UK citizens living elsewhere in the European Union, and we should aim to strike an early agreement about their rights.

16. We should work towards securing a comprehensive agreement. We want to agree a deep and special partnership between the UK and the EU, taking in both economic and security cooperation. We will need to discuss how we determine a fair settlement of the UK's rights and obligations as a departing member state, in accordance with the law and in the spirit of the United Kingdom's continuing partnership with the EU. But we believe it is necessary to agree the terms of our future partnership alongside those of our withdrawal from the EU.

17. We should work together to minimize disruption and give as much certainty as possible. Investors, businesses and citizens in both the UK and across the remaining 27 member states — and

those from third countries around the world — want to be able to plan. In order to avoid any cliff-edge as we move from our current relationship to our future partnership, people and businesses in both the UK and the EU would benefit from implementation periods to adjust in a smooth and orderly way to new arrangements. It would help both sides to minimize unnecessary disruption if we agree this principle early in the process.

18. In particular, we must pay attention to the UK's unique relationship with the Republic of Ireland and the importance of the peace process in Northern Ireland. The Republic of Ireland is the only EU member state with a land border with the United Kingdom. We want to avoid a return to a hard border between our two countries, to be able to maintain the Common Travel Area between us, and to make sure that the UK's withdrawal from the EU does not harm the Republic of Ireland. We also have an important responsibility to make sure that nothing is done to jeopardize the peace process in Northern Ireland, and to continue to uphold the Belfast Agreement.

19. We should begin technical talks on detailed policy areas as soon as possible, but we should priorities the biggest challenges. Agreeing a high-level approach to the issues arising from our withdrawal will of course be an early priority. But we also propose a bold and ambitious Free Trade Agreement between the United Kingdom and the European Union. This should be of greater scope and ambition than any such agreement before it so that it covers sectors crucial to our linked economies such as financial services and network industries. This will require detailed technical talks, but as the UK is an existing EU member state, both sides have regulatory frameworks and standards that already match. We should therefore prioritize how we manage the evolution of our regulatory frameworks to maintain a fair and open trading environment, and how we resolve disputes. On the scope of the partnership between us — on both economic and security matters — my officials will put forward detailed proposals for deep, broad and dynamic cooperation.

20. We should continue to work together to advance and protect our shared European values. Perhaps now more than ever, the world needs the liberal, democratic values of Europe. We want to play our part to ensure that Europe remains strong and prosperous and able to lead in the world, projecting its values and defending itself from security threats.

THE TASK BEFORE US

21. As I have said, the Government of the United Kingdom wants to agree a deep and special partnership between the UK and the EU, taking in both economic and security cooperation. At a time when the growth of global trade is slowing and there are signs that protectionist instincts are on the rise in many parts of the world, Europe has a responsibility to stand up for free trade in the interest of all our citizens. Likewise, Europe's security is more fragile today than at any time since the end of the Cold War. Weakening our cooperation for the prosperity and protection of our citizens would be a costly mistake. The United Kingdom's objectives for our future partnership remain those set out in my Lancaster House speech of 17 January and the subsequent White Paper published on 2 February.

22. We recognize that it will be a challenge to reach such a comprehensive agreement within the two-year period set out for withdrawal discussions in the Treaty. But we believe it is necessary to agree the terms of our future partnership alongside those of our withdrawal from the EU. We start from a unique position in these discussions — close regulatory alignment, trust in one another's institutions, and a spirit of cooperation stretching back decades. It is for these reasons, and because the future partnership between the UK and the EU is of such importance to both sides, that I am sure it can be agreed in the time period set out by the Treaty.

23. The task before us is momentous but it should not be beyond us. After all, the institutions and the leaders of the European Union have succeeded in bringing together a continent blighted by war into a union of peaceful nations, and supported the transition of dictatorships to democracy. Together, I know we are capable of reaching an agreement about the UK's rights and obligations as a departing member state, while establishing a deep and special partnership that contributes towards the prosperity, security and global power of our continent. Courtesy: (Prime Minister's Office, 10 Downing Street Department for Exiting the European Union. The RT Hon Theresa May MP. 29 March 2017).

BIBLIOGRAPHY

Ablon L. Libicki, MC and Golay, AA .2014.*Markets for Cybercrime Tools and Stolen Data: Hackers Bazaar'*. Santa Monica, CA, Rand Corporation.

Anderson, R. Bohme, R, Clayton. R and Moore, T. 2008. *Security Economics and the Internal Market*. European Network and Information Security Agency

Ackerman, Bruce 2006. *Before the next attack: preserving civil liberties in an age of terrorism*, New Haven, CT and London: Yale University Press

Anderson D.M and Killingray D, 1992, *Policing and decolonization: Politics, nationalism and the police 1917-965*, Manchester University Press

Argomaniz, Javier. 2011. *The EU and Counter-Terrorism. Politics, polity and policies after 9/11* London and New York: Routledge

Adey, Peter and Ben Anderson 2012. Anticipating emergencies: Technologies of preparedness and the matter of security, *Security Dialogue*

Archibald, M.E, Patrick Colquhoun, 1745-1820. *A history of the Lothian and border police*, Scotland Military Collectors Society, 1990

Alberts, David S, John J. Garstka, Frederick P. Stein, 1999, *Network Centric Warfare: Developing and Leveraging Information Superiority*. Washington DC: C4ISR Cooperative Research Program

Aldrich, R.J. (2004) 'Transatlantic intelligence and security co-operation.' *International Affairs*, Vol. 80

Agrell, Wilhelm. 2002. 'When everything is intelligence — nothing is intelligence', The Sherman Kent Center for Intelligence *Analysis Occasional Papers*, 1,

Acton, James M. 2014. 'International Verification and Intelligence', *Intelligence and National Security journal, Vol. 29*

Aid, Matthew M, 2003, 'All Glory is Fleeting: Sigint and the Fight against International Terrorism', *Intelligence and National Security journal, Vol. 18*

Andrew, Christopher and Mitrokhin, Vasili, 2005, *The World Was Going Our Way: The KGB and the Battle for the Third World*. New York: Basic Books

Ascher K. 1987, *the Politics of Privatization*, Macmillan, London

Akkad O. 2006, 'Muslim Teen Seeks Belief in Its Perfect Form.' *Globe and Mail*

Amghar S., Boubekeur A. and Emerson M. 2007, *European Islam: Challenges for Society and Public Policy*, Centre for European Policy Studies. Brussels

Aldrich, R.J. 2004 'Transatlantic Intelligence and Security Co-operation'. *International Affairs Journal, Vol. 80, No. 4*

Argomaniz J, 2011. *The EU and Counter-Terrorism: Politics, polity and policies after 9/11*, London and New York: Routledge

Alexander, Yonah and Edgar H. Brenner 2000.*Legal aspects of terrorism in the United States*. Dobbs Ferry, N.Y. Oceana Publications

Allan, Richard. 1990. *Terrorism: pragmatic international deterrence and cooperation*. New York Institute for East West Security Studies

Ahemd, Samina. 1999. 'Pakistan's Nuclear Weapons Programme: Turning Points and Nuclear Choices,' *International Security*

Amin, Thahir. February 1993. 'Pakistan in 1993: Some Dramatic Changes,' *Asian Survey*

Auner, Aric. February 2010. 'Pakistani Nuclear Weapons Now Under PM,' *Arms Control Today, Vol. 40*

Alain, M. 2001, 'the Trapeze Artists and the Ground Crew Police Cooperation and Intelligence Exchange Mechanisms in Europe and North America: a Comparative Empirical Study'. *Policing and Society, 2001, Vol.11*

Andrew, Christopher and Oleg Gordievsky, 1990, *KGB, the Inside Story of Its Foreign Operations from Lenin to Gorbachev*, London: Hodder & Stoughton

Bamford James. 2002. *Body of Secrets. How America's NSA and Brittan's GCHQ Eavesdrop on the World*. Arrow Books, London

Banerji Rana, October 2011. Pakistan: 'Inter-Services Intelligence Directorate (ISI). An Analytical Overview', *Journal of Defense Studies*

Barrie D.G, 2010, 'A Topology of British Police-Locating the Scottish Municipal Police Model in its British context 1800–1835.' *British Journal of Criminology*

Barnad C. 2011. *Using procurement law to enforce labor standards*, Oxford University Press Blakeslee, MR. 2012. *Internet Crimes, Torts and Scams: Investigation and Remedies*. Oxford: Oxford University Press

Bleaken, D. 2010. 'Botwars: the Fight against Criminal Cyber Networks.' *Computer Fraud and Security*

Bossler, AM and Holt, 1J. 2009. 'On-line Activities, Guardianship, and Malware Infection: An Examination of Routine Activities Theory.' *International Journal of Cyber Criminology*

Bean, H. 2007, 'The DNI's Open Source Centre: An Organizational Communication Perspective'. *International Journal of Intelligence and Counterintelligence, Vol. 20, No. 2*

Beckley A. 20 January, 1995. 'Biting the Bullet', *Police Review*

Beach, D. 2005, *The Dynamics of European integration: why and when EU institutions matter*, Palgrave Macmillan.

Beckman, James, 2007, *Comparative Legal Approaches to Homeland Security and Anti-Terrorism Homeland Security Series*, Ashgate London

Bennett Richard. 2002. *Espionage, Spies & Secrets*, Virgin Books, London

Bergeron, Kenneth D.. 2002, *Tritium on Ice: The Dangerous New Alliance of Nuclear Weapons and Nuclear Power*. Cambridge, MIT Press.

Betts, Richard. 2007. *Enemies of Intelligence: Knowledge and Power in American National Security*, Columbia University Press

Bochel, H., Defty, A. and Dunn, A. 2010, *scrutinizing the Secret State: parliamentary oversight of the intelligence and security agencies.* Policy & Politics

Bochel, H. Defty, A. and Kirkpatrick, J. 2014, *Watching the Watchers Parliament and the Intelligence Services.* Palgrave Macmillan.

Braga Anthony A. 2008, *Police Enforcement Strategies to Prevent Crime in Hot Spot Area, Crime and Prevention Research Review, Program in Criminal Justice and Management*, John F. Kennedy School of Government, Harvard University.

Brandon, James August 2015, 'Rise of Islamic State Reignites British Radicalization Threat'. *Terrorism Monitor*

Brewer John.D and Gareth. 1998. *Northern Ireland, 1921-1998*, Macmillan Press, London

Bretherton, Charlotte and John Vogler, 2004.*The European Union as a Global Actor*, London, Routledge

Bruce S. 1992. *The Red Hand: Protestant paramilitaries in Northern Ireland*, Oxford University Press.

Bunyan T. 1977. *The History and Practice of the Political Police in Britain*, London Quartet Books

Buckley A. and Kenny M.C. 1995, *Negotiating Identity: Rhetoric, Metaphor and social drama in Northern Ireland*, Smithsonian Institute Press

Caldicott, Helen. 2002, *The New Nuclear Danger: George W. Bush's Military-Industrial Complex*. New York: The New Press

Cameron, Fraser, 1999. *The Foreign and Security Policy of the European Union: Past, Present and Future,* Sheffield Academy

Carlsnaes, Walter and Steve Smith. 1994, *European Foreign Policy: The EC and Changing Foreign Policy Perspectives in Europe, London:* Sage

Carlsnaes, Walter, Helene Sjursen, and Brian White. 2004, *Contemporary European Foreign Policy,* London: Sage.

Castagna, Michael, 1997, 'Virtual Intelligence: Reengineering Doctrine for the Information Age' *International Journal of Intelligence and Counterintelligence,* 10, 2

Chase, Alston, 2003. *Harvard and the Unabomber: The Education of an American Terrorist.* New York: W. W. Norton.

Chesterman, S. 2006, 'Does the UN Have Intelligence'? *Survival, Vol. 48, No. 3, autumn, London*

Chomsky, Noam. 1988. *The culture of terrorism.* South End Press.

Clarke, James W. 2012, *Defining Danger: American Assassins and the New Domestic Terrorists.* New Brunswick: Transaction Publishers

Combs, Cindy C. 1997.*Terrorism in the twenty first century.* Prentice Hall

Cooley, John K. 1990. *Unholy wars: Afghanistan, America, and international terrorism.* Pluto Press, 1999 Crelinsten, Ronald D. 1978. *Terrorism and criminal justice: an international perspective.* Lexington Books

Coolsaet, R. 2010, 'EU Counter-terrorism strategy: Value-added or chimera?' *International Affairs, Vol. 86, No. 4*

Coolsaet, Rik. 2011, *Jihadi Terrorism and the Radicalization Challenge: European and American Experiences.* Farnham: Ashgate.

Cooper, Robert, 2003. *The Breaking of Nations: Order and Chaos in the Twenty-First Century,* Atlantic Books.

Coulter C. 1997, *Contemporary Northern Irish Society: An Introduction,* Pluto Press, London.

Crawford C. 2003, *Inside the UDA: Volunteers and Violence,* Pluto Press, London.

Crenshaw Martha. 1983. *Terrorism, legitimacy, and power: the consequences of political violence.* Middletown, Conn. Wesleyan University Press

Crowe, Brian, May 2003. 'Europe's CFSP after Iraq', *International Affairs, vol. 79, no. 3*

Davis, Jack. 2002. Improving CIA Analytic Performance: DI Analytic Priorities'. Sherman Kent Center for Intelligence Analysis, *Occasional Papers, Vol.1, no. 3.* Washington, DC

Dingledine, R & Mathewson, N. 2006. 'Anonymity Loves Company: Usability and the Network Effect'. *Paper presented at the 5th Workshop on the Economics of Information Security,* Cambridge, UK.

Dockrill, Michael L and David French. 1996, *Strategy and Intelligence: British Policy during the First World War*. Rio Grande, OH: Hambledon Press

Douglas Hay, Francis G. Snyder, 1989, *Policing and prosecution in Britain, 1750-1850*, Clarendon Press.

Duefer, Charles. 2009. 'Hide and Seek: The Search for Truth in Iraq'. *Public Affairs*, New York.

Eliassen, Kjell. 1998. *Foreign and Security Policy in the European Union*, London: Sage

Elliott, S. and W.D, Flakes. 1999, *Northern Ireland, A Political Dictionary, 1968-1999*, Belfast, Blackstaff Press

Ellison Graham, and Smyth Jim, 2000, *the Crowned Harp: Policing Northern Ireland*, Pluto Press, London

English, Richard, 2003, *Armed Struggle: A History of IRA*, MacMillan, London

Evan. G. and Duffy M. 1997, 'Beyond the Sectarian Divide: The social Bases and Political consequences of Nationalist and Unionist Party Competition in Northern Ireland'. *British Journal of Political Science*

Fair C. Christine. 2007. 'Militant Recruitment in Pakistan: A New Look at the Militancy-Madrasa-Connection', *Asian Policy*.

Felson, M and Clarke, RV. 1998. 'Opportunity Makes the Thief: Practical Theory for Crime Prevention. *Police Research Series Paper 98'. London: Policing and Reducing Crime Unit, Home Office.

Ferguson Charles D, William C. Potter. 2004. 'The Four Faces of Nuclear Terrorism', *Monterey Institute of International Studies*.

Fingar T. 2011. *Reducing uncertainty: intelligence analysis and national security*, Stanford University Press

Frank P. Harvey. 2008. *The Homeland Security Dilemma: Fear, Failure and the Future of American Insecurity*. Routledge, London.

Friedrichs J, 2008, *Fighting Terrorism and Drugs, Europe and international police cooperation*, London and New York: Routledge

Frost, Robin M. 2005. *Nuclear terrorism after 9/11, Abingdon*: Routledge for the International Institute for Strategic Studies.

Ganguli Sumit and Devin T. Hagerty. 2006. *Fearful Symmetry: India-Pakistan Crisis in the Shadow of Nuclear Weapons*. Seattle, W.A, University of Washington Press.

Ganguli Sumit and S. Paul Kapur. 2009. *Nuclear Proliferation in South Asia: Crisis Behavior and the Bomb*. Routledge, New York.

Gavin, Francis J. 2012. *Nuclear statecraft: history and strategy in America's atomic age*. Cornell University Press

Gibson, David R. 2012. *Talk at the brink: deliberation and decision during the Cuban Missile Crisis.* Princeton: Princeton University Press.

Ginsberg, Roy, 2001. *The European Union in International Politics: Baptism by Fire,* Lanham, Rowman and Littlefield

Gomez, Ricardo and John Peterson, Spring 2001. 'The EU's Impossibly Busy Foreign Ministers: 'No One is in Control', *European Foreign Affairs Review, vol. 6, no. 1*

Han, Henry Hyunwook. 1993. *Terrorism & Political Violence: Limits & Possibilities of Legal Control,* Oceana Publications, New York, US

Harvey, Frank P. 2008. 'The Homeland Security Dilemma: Fear, Failure, and the Future of American Insecurity'. *Contemporary Security Studies*

Hillebrand, Claudia, 2012, *Counter-Terrorism Networks in the European Union: Maintaining Democratic Legitimacy after 9/11.* Oxford: Oxford University Press

Hoffman, Bruce; Reinares, Fernando 2014, *The Evolution of the Global Terrorist Threat: From 9/11 to Osama bin Laden's Death. Columbia Studies in Terrorism and Irregular Warfare,* New York, Columbia University Press

Howie, Luke. 2012. *Witnesses to terror: understanding the meanings and consequences of terrorism.* Basingstoke: Palgrave Macmillan

Howitt, Arnold M. 2003. *Countering terrorism: dimensions of preparedness.* Cambridge, Mass.: MIT Press.

'Intelligence Organizations in Combating Armed Groups', *Journal of Public and International Affairs, 2,* Princeton: Princeton University Press, 2001.

Jervis, Robert. Spring 1986. 'What's wrong with the Intelligence Process'? *International Journal of Intelligence and Counterintelligence 1, no. 2*

Johnson, Douglas H.. 2004-2010. 'Sources of Intelligence: A Bibliography of the Monthly Sudan' *Intelligence Report. Volume 11, Number-1, Northeast African studies*

Johnson, Loch. 1989, *Seven Sins of Strategic Intelligence, in America's Secret Power: The CIA in a democratic Society,* New York: Oxford University Press

Johnson, Loch. 2004. 'The Aspin-Brown Intelligence Inquiry: Behind the Closed Doors of a Blue Ribbon Commission', *Studies in Intelligence 48, no. 3*

Johnston, Les. 1999, *Policing in Britain, Longman Criminology Series,* Longman.

Kent, Sherman, 1966. *Strategic Intelligence for American World Policy.* Princeton University Press, 1966

Khan Saira. 2009. *Nuclear Weapons and Conflict Transformation, the Case of India-Pakistan.* Routledge Taylor and Francis Group, London.

Krepton Michael. 2009. *Better Safe than Sorry: The Ironies of Living with the Bomb.* Stanford University Press, USA.

Krotz Ulrich and Schild Joachim, 2013.*Shaping Europe: France, Germany, and Embedded Bilateralism from the Elysee Treaty to Twenty-First Century Politics.* Oxford University Press, UK.

Lan Bellany. 2007. *Terrorism and Weapons of Mass Destruction: Responding to the Challenge.* Routledge, London

Lawday, David. 2000, *policing in France and Britain, Restoring confidence locally and nationally,* Franco-British council. London

Lewis Jeffrey. 2014. *Paper Tiger: China's Nuclear Posture.* International Institute for Strategic Studies, London

Lian W. 2010. 'Talibanization in the Tribal Area of Pakistan', *Journal of Middle Eastern and Islamic Studies.*

Luongo, Kenneth N. and Naeem Salik, December, 1, 2007. 'Building Confidence in Pakistan's Nuclear Security', *Arms Control Today.*

Mawby, Rob and Dr Alan Wright, 2005, *Police Accountability in the United Kingdom.*Keele University, UK

McCarthy, Mary. Spring 1994. 'The National Warning System: Striving for an Elusive Goal,' *Defense Intelligence Journal 3, no. 1*

Messervy-Whiting, G. 2004, *Intelligence Cooperation in the European Union, Centre for Studies in Security and Diplomacy,* University of Birmingham,

Muller-Wille, Bjorn, January 2004. 'For your eyes only? Shaping an intelligence community within the EU', *Occasional Papers, Institute for Security Studies,* No.50

Nomikos, John M. June 2005. 'The European Union's Proposed Intelligence Service', *PINR,*

Odom, William E. 2003, *Fixing Intelligence: for a More Secure America.* New Haven: Yale University Press

Omand, David. 2010. *Securing the State.* Hurst & Company London

Orr-Munro T. 28 March 2000, 'Women at arms', *Police Review*

Perrow, Charles. 1984, *Normal Accidents: Living with High-Risk Technologies.* New York: Basic Books

Ronczkowski, M.R. 2006, *Terrorism and Organized Hate Crime: Intelligence Gathering, Analysis, and Investigations.* CRC Press, Boca Raton, Florida, US

Schmid, A. P. 2011. *The Routledge handbook of terrorism research.* New York: Routledge.

Silke, A., ed. 2004. *Research on terrorism: Trends, achievements and failures.* London: Frank Cass.

Smith, M. L. R. 1996, *Fighting for Ireland: The Military Strategy of the Irish Republican Movement.* London: Routledge

Smithson, Amy E. and Leslie-Anne Levy. October 2000. *Ataxia: The Chemical and Biological Threat and the US Response. Report no. 35*, Henry L. Stimson Center

Stefik, Mark and Barbara Stefik, 2004, *Breakthrough: Stories and Strategies of Radical Innovation*. Cambridge, MA: MIT Press

Stern, Jessica. 1999, *the Ultimate Terrorists*. Cambridge: Harvard University Press

Stevenson, Jonathan. Winter 2003-04. 'Africa's Growing Strategic Resonance'. *Survival, vol. 45, no. 4,*

Timmerman, Kenneth R.2003, *Preachers of Hate: Islam and the War on America*. Random House, New York

Toolis, Kevin. 1996, Rebel *Hearts: Journeys within the IRA' Soul*. St. Martin's Press

Travers, Russ. 1996, 'the Coming Intelligence Failure', *Studies in Intelligence 40, no. 2*

Tucker, Jonathan B. 2000, *Toxic Terror: Assessing Terrorist Use of Chemical and Biological Weapons*. Cambridge: MIT Press

Tucker, Jonathan B. and Robert P. Kadlec, 2001. 'Infectious Disease and National Security', *Strategic Review, vol. 29, no. 2*

Van Bruinessen, Martin. 2002. Genealogies of Islamic Radicalism in post-Suharto Indonesia', *South East Research, vol. 10, no. 2*

Varshney, Ashutosh. 2002, *Competing National Imaginations, in Ethnic Conflict and Civic Life: Hindus and Muslims in India*. New Haven: Yale University Press

Volpi, Frederic. 2008. *Transnational Islam and Regional Security*, Routledge, London.

Walsh, Patrick F.. 2011. *Intelligence and intelligence analysis*. Routledge, Taylor and Francis, London.

Weinberg, L. 2005. *Global terrorism: A beginner's guide*. Oxford: One world.

Wellock Thomas R. 1998. *Opposition to Nuclear Power in California, 1958-1978*. Madison, University of Wisconsin Press

Wenger Andreas and Wollenmann Reto. 2007. *Bioterrorism: Confronting a Complete Threat*. Lynne Rienner Publishers London.

Whitaker, D. J. 2007. *Terrorism reader*, London, Routledge

Whitney Craig R. 2005. 'The WMD Mirage: Iraq's Decade of Deception and America's False Premises for War', *Journal of Public Affairs*, New York

Wilkinson, P. 2000. *The Strategic Implications of Terrorism. Terrorism and Political Violence*. Haranand Publications, India

Yensen H. 12 March 1995, Gun and Law, Bad Lore, *Police Review*

Yoshihara Toshi and James R. Holmes, 2012, *Strategy in the Second Nuclear Age: Power Ambitions and the Ultimate Weapon*. Georgetown University Washington DC

Young J. 1999, *the Exclusive Society*, Sage Publishing Company

Zaeef, Abdul Salam, *My Life with the Taliban*, London: Hurst and Company, 2009.

Zahab, Mariam Abu, and Olivier Roy, 2004, *Islamist Networks: The Afghan-Pakistan Connection*, London: C. Hurst Books

Printed in the United States
By Bookmasters